METHODISM AND THE LITERATURE
OF THE EIGHTEENTH CENTURY

METHODISM AND THE LITERATURE OF THE EIGHTEENTH CENTURY

BY

T. B. SHEPHERD, M.A., Ph.D.

THE EPWORTH PRESS
(EDGAR C. BARTON)
25-35 CITY ROAD, LONDON, E.C.1

Made in Great Britain

TO

THE REV. DR. AND MRS. A. W. HARRISON

PREFACE

T<small>HIS</small> study is the shortened form of a thesis approved for the degree of Doctor of Philosophy in the University of London, and its publication has been aided by grants from the University Publication Fund and from the Publication Fund of Birkbeck College.

I am particularly indebted to the heads of the English School at Birkbeck College: the late Mr. J. H. Lobban, through whose inspiration and encouragement I began this work, and Professor J. R. Sutherland for his constant advice and criticism. Here should follow a lengthy catalogue of friends who have given me information and to whom I am most grateful, but I must confine myself to mentioning Dr. E. C. Batho and the Principal, Staff, and many students of Westminster College.

Any writer on Methodism and Literature must be indebted to the careful research of the Wesley Historical Society and to the works of Dr. Henry Bett and the Rev. F. C. Gill. I ask for their forgiveness if at any time I have not acknowledged my debts in the footnotes.

Finally, may I add that for the imperfections of this book and all its errors of fact or judgement I am solely responsible.

T. B. S<small>HEPHERD</small>

W<small>ESTMINSTER</small> C<small>OLLEGE</small>
May 14th, 1940

PREFACE TO SECOND EDITION

SHORTLY after the appearance of the first edition of this book most of the copies were destroyed in the great fires caused by the air-raids. In true Methodist tradition, however, a brand was plucked from the burning, and I hope it may still throw some light on the eighteenth century.

I am indebted to many friends who have pointed out a number of errors which have been corrected in this new edition. Some footnotes have been amplified and the bibliography brought up to date, but otherwise the book remains the same as in 1940.

T. B. SHEPHERD

October 1946

CONTENTS

INTRODUCTION

In recent years social historians have stressed the importance of the Methodist movement on English life. They have suggested that it had much to do with the increase in humanitarian ideas, liberal opinions, and the rise of the working-class movements. Little, however, has been written about the literary importance of Methodism, though critics have agreed upon the value of Wesley's *Journal*, and some have recognized Charles Wesley as a poet of distinction. Recently there has also been some investigation into the influence of Methodism on the Romantic Revival. It is the purpose of this book to examine the whole subject of the place of Methodism in the literature of the eighteenth century. This falls easily into three sections.

The first deals with the literary work of the Wesleys themselves. Enough quotations are given to illustrate their powers as prose and verse writers, and their critical views are examined. The second section deals with the works of other Methodist writers, and the third with the attitude of the literary men of the time towards the new movement.

Throughout the book the theological side of the movement and the religious controversies are overlooked as far as possible, though in estimating the importance of Methodism on the national life it is impossible totally to disregard its theology. Before beginning to examine any of Wesley's works in detail, some short account of the man himself may be given, though this can be brief, on account of the great number of excellent biographies that are available. Some points about the origins and influence of the Methodist movement are of such importance to the whole subject to be considered that they will be emphasized here.

John Wesley was born on June 28, 1703, being the fifteenth

child of the Rev. Samuel and Susanna Wesley. His father, a strong High Churchman and Tory, was the Rector of Epworth in Lincolnshire. His living was small, and on account of his political activities and his addiction to writing and publishing verse, he was constantly in debt and sometime in prison. It was to his mother, however, that John Wesley owed most, for she was an outstanding woman of great sincerity and charm, always calm, ordered, and logical. She had nineteen children and reared nine of them, believing in strict discipline, insisting always on good manners and courtesy and always being cheerful herself. Wesley seems to have inherited or learned all these characteristics from her, and they remained with him all his life.

In 1714 he was admitted to Charterhouse on the nomination of the Duke of Buckingham, and in 1720 left there with a scholarship of £40 to carry him to Christ Church, Oxford, as a Commoner. While at Oxford he began to keep a diary in cipher, noting down what he did from hour to hour. This is of interest because it proves that he led the ordinary kind of life of a student of the period. He read widely, played tennis, took long walks, swam, rowed on the river, and was sometimes 'treated at the Coffee House and Tennis Court'. In 1725 he decided on the Church for a career, was ordained by the Bishop of Oxford, and returned to help his father at Epworth both in making sermons and in working on his great commentary on the Book of Job. In 1726, he was elected a Fellow of Lincoln and returned to Oxford to preside over the daily disputations and to teach Greek. In 1727 he took his Master's degree and read Hebrew, Arabic, Metaphysics, Natural Philosophy, Poetry, and Divinity. Two years later he joined a group of young men who met on certain evenings to study the Classics and the Bible, for devotion, and to make plans for social service. He soon became the leader of this group, which increased in numbers, so that it became widely known.

Great scandal was caused in Oxford because they attended Holy Communion once a week, while most churchmen considered that three times a year was quite satisfactory.

The lives of those who met with Wesley were regularized: they began to cut themselves off from worldly pleasures, to eat little, to rise early, to fill every moment of the day with work or with 'good works'. They gave all they could to the poor and to the prisoners and sick whom they visited. Wesley himself seems to have tried to find a personal 'salvation' in this life of asceticism, with its monastic regularity. This religious group soon became noted in Oxford, and it was given such nicknames as Bible Moths, the Holy Club, Methodists. The term 'Methodist' had been used in the previous century of certain medical schools and of groups of Puritans, but it seems extremely likely that it was simply given them because of the stress on the regularity and method of the lives of the members. The term was carried over later on to the followers of John Wesley when he began field preaching. It is sometimes, however, forgotten that the success of the movement later was largely due to the method and organization of John Wesley, and the madness attributed to him and to his followers was originally on account of this regularity and insistence on order and method in religious life. It is easy to forget that the eighteenth-century gentleman who snorted at 'enthusiasm' when he saw the Methodists did not necessarily imply that they were wild, uneducated ranters. The term was often loosely used to describe the behaviour or beliefs of any one with whom one disagreed, just as 'Bolshevism' is used to-day. No one ever called himself an Enthusiast. Wesley defined *enthusiasm* in his *Dictionary* as *religious madness* or *fancied inspiration*; Dr. Johnson called it 'A vain belief of private revelation; a vain confidence of divine favour or communication'; Locke spoke of it as 'the conceits of a warmed, or overweening brain'.[1] Thus, if a preacher was an 'enthusiast' he spoke with too great authority or falsely claimed inspiration, he suggested too much emphasis on certain subjects, or was too insistent on morality or doctrine, but he did not of necessity shout or rant, or behave outwardly differently

[1] In the essay on 'Superstition and Enthusiasm,' David Hume wrote: 'Hope, pride, presumption, a warm imagination, together with ignorance are the true sources of Enthusiasm' (*The Philosophical Works of David Hume*, T. H. Green, 1872, vol. iii, p. 145).

from any other clergyman. 'Enthusiasm' was the substance, not the manner of preaching. To the ordinary man, however, any peculiar beliefs or behaviour were 'enthusiasm'.

For the next six years Wesley remained at Oxford as a tutor, doing the ordinary duties of a Fellow with far more than common insistence and industry, as some of his pupils complained. His attempts to find 'salvation' by 'works', however, failed, and in 1735 he accepted an invitation to go to the new colony of Georgia as a missionary. His brother Charles also went as secretary to General Oglethorpe, the founder of the venture to transplant debtors, prisoners, and religious exiles to America to colonize this particular district. Before leaving, John presented his father's great Latin folio on Job to Queen Caroline, who thanked him very pleasantly and said, 'It is very prettily bound'.

Wesley began his *Journal* when he sailed for Georgia, probably writing up his general accounts each evening before going to bed. He afterwards published all the section about the American adventure as a justification of his conduct there. The rugged side of his life at this period is often neglected: he worked in semi-tropical heat, stripped to the waist, building huts, cutting trees, and planting gardens. He trekked through forests and swamps, and crossed rivers and lakes in frail boats: he found no Indians who could be trusted and none who would be converted. The white settlers, too, were the dregs of society, and Wesley's methods, though courageous and thorough, were not tactful. He rebuked those who did wrong, told each truthfully and clearly his faults, and tried to enforce the most rigid rules of the Church of England. He seems to have discovered and revived some that other men had sensibly forgotten, as, for example, that of complete immersion at baptism. He made many enemies who attacked him violently and brought lawsuits against him, and he was once nearly murdered by a furious woman. He offended the settlers by uncompromising resistance to slavery, proving by his own hard labour that white men could work in that climate, despite all arguments to the contrary. George Whitefield a year or so later visited Georgia, had no objections to slavery, was not nearly so rigid in his behaviour, and was a great success. In 1737 Wesley had a law suit still dragging on, was attacked maliciously on all sides, and, after due warning, returned to England.

On the journeys to and from America and in Georgia he was greatly impressed with the fearless behaviour of the German Moravians, and on returning to England began to investigate them still further. Certain more devout members of the Church of England during the early eighteenth century met together in religious societies, and Wesley began to visit one in Fetter Lane, at which English Moravians, who were at that time discussing with bishops the possibility of joining with the Church of England, also attended. He greatly admired their lack of fear, their serenity, their orderly habits, and their certainty about salvation, though he was critical of their belief in Stillness or Quietism, and hostile to their disregard of the Sacraments. They laid great stress on the fact that salvation was not by works, from which Wesley had been vainly seeking it, but that it was an inner experience of faith, and that belief in this gave men peace, certainty, and joy. Wesley began to seek this.

To many great religious leaders vital experiences have come suddenly, or have culminated suddenly, and on May 24, 1738, Wesley went 'very unwillingly' to a meeting house in Aldersgate Street. Here, after hearing Luther's *Preface to the Epistle to the Romans* read, at 'about a quarter to nine', he 'felt his heart strangely warmed'. The Evangelical movement of the century is generally dated from this moment, and it is frequently termed Wesley's 'conversion'. This certainly serves as a name for a vital experience, though it was some months before he had that power of preaching derived from complete faith and serenity, and felt the burning call to tell others of the possibility of such joy on this earth. The experience, however, is of a different character from that of the general, psychological use of the word, where a man is overwhelmed by his sense of sin and hopelessness, which comes to a crisis that is possibly physical as well as mental. The convert may possibly suffer from abnormalities, see visions or drop into a trance, but, after a great crisis, will suddenly find relief, followed by a tremendous reaction of peace or joy. This is the general system of conversions, which only come dramatically to certain types of mind.

George Whitefield returned in December, 1738, after a triumphant success in America. Only twenty-five years old, he was already a great dramatic orator and preached with great power; but he was labelled 'an enthusiast', and certain churches were closed to him. He had few of Wesley's rigid and set views about Church authority, and where he saw great crowds anxious to hear his gospel, but with no church to go to or no church that he could preach in, he began to speak in the open air. John Wesley was greatly shocked. Then churches were closed against him also, because he seemed too certain and too 'enthusiastic' in doctrine. Moreover, the tales of the dangerous 'enthusiasm' of Oxford and of weekly Holy Communion lived on. Whitefield had gone to Bristol, and rumours came to London of his preaching to as many as 10,000 at once, and of crowds of un-educated and wild colliers asking for religion. Seeing that something more than emotional preaching was needed and that a leader with organizing power was necessary, he wrote and urged Wesley to join him. Wesley greatly disliked the idea; for his ideal was the regular service of the Church of England or a devotional meeting of earnest and intelligent men and women. He consulted his brother Charles, who, in addition to having much less sense than his brother, was much more devoted to legal forms of Churchmanship and much more snobbish. Charles was against John's leaving London. John hated the idea of preaching out of a church; he desired 'to live and die in seclusion', yet the bishops and regular clergy did nothing for these thousands. He had gone to America to preach to Indians who did not want him: here were Englishmen asking for him. When in difficulty he resorted to what may be called a wholly superstitious practice, but one commonly used by Moravians and indeed by many others at that time. He opened the Bible at random and read the first words for guidance. The numerous times on which it was no help never seemed to deter him, and he seemed to make up his own mind about what it meant afterwards. Should he go and join Whitefield at Bristol? The answer was: 'Now there was long war between the House of Saul and the House of David.' Wesley decided to go to Bristol and thus began his fifty-two years of preaching and travel.

Probably the most able Churchman of the time was Bishop Butler, whose *Analogy of Religion* was published in 1736 and who was appointed Bishop of Bristol in 1738, about the time when the field preaching of Whitefield and Wesley was beginning. He was greatly disturbed by the 'enthusiasm' he saw springing up in his diocese, and must have heard strange stories of Methodists preaching in the open to crowds of the colliers of Kingswood, who were little better than semi-savages. He asked Wesley to come and see him, and both men tried to explain their points of view. The interview has often been quoted, but is of great interest, because both were sincere and Butler represents the orthodox view of the time. Butler also was not, like many of his time, attacking Wesley for stupid reasons and asserting that he was a Jacobite, a Papist or a Quaker. Towards the end of the interview he said:

Mr. Wesley, I will deal plainly with you. I once thought you and Mr. Whitefield well-meaning men; but I cannot think so now. For I have heard more of you: matters of fact, sir. And Mr. Whitefield says in his *Journal*: 'There are promises still to be fulfilled in me.' Sir, the pretending to extraordinary revelations and gifts of the Holy Ghost is a horrid thing—a very horrid thing!

Wesley: My lord, for what Mr. Whitefield says, Mr. Whitefield, and not I, is accountable. I pretend to no extraordinary revelations or gifts of the Holy Ghost: none but what every Christian may receive and ought to expect and pray for.

At the end of the interview, Butler said:

Sir, you have no business here: you are not commissioned to preach in this diocese: therefore I advise you to go hence.[1]

Wesley, however, continued to preach there, though he always had a high opinion of Butler and of 'that fine book, Bishop Butler's *Analogy*', which he read several times.

This new kind of life did not well agree with the doctrines

[1] See *Journal*, vol. ii, p. 257.

of Stillness upheld at the Religious Society at Fetter Lane, and in 1740 the Wesleys separated from it. Later this Society broke away from the Church of England and became a Church of the Moravians. The birth of the real Methodist societies, as distinct from certain people preaching in the open air, is interesting. In 1739 a number of people came to Wesley and told him they wanted to form a religious society of their own, and placed themselves under his control. He agreed to meet them every Thursday evening when possible. Their numbers increased, and, as Wesley was practical, they were sent to visit the poor and help those who were ill. To pay expenses, those who could paid a penny each week, and some of them became stewards and collected this. More room was needed, so the ruins of an old gun-foundry were bought and a meeting place erected near Finsbury Square. A school for poor children was started and what was probably the first dispensary for medicines was set up.[1] Another place was bought for those wishing to meet Wesley at Bristol, and a little later another at Newcastle. The movement grew and there came an evolution of rules, tickets of membership, and insistence on strict standards of conduct, charity, and education. Wesley visited his societies, preaching at different places on his journeys, and other societies and classes were founded.

Few people took notice of this side, the important side, of the movement; for most of the attention centred on the dramatic preaching of George Whitefield. Clergymen objected to field preaching, especially when so many attended and so little regard was paid to themselves. Educated and orthodox people objected to the emotional scenes and the frantic behaviour of some people who listened. The more practical, conservative opinion foresaw social dangers: for, if the poor thought they had souls, would they not want better conditions and higher wages? A correspondent, for example, wrote to the *Gentleman's Magazine* fearing to 'hear of a prodigious Rise in the Price of Coals about the City of Bristol' because of these 'Methodists'. Great ladies were offended at the preaching about sin. The Duchess of

[1] See *London in the Eighteenth Century*, by M. D. George.

Buckingham protested: 'It is monstrous to be told that you have a heart as *sinful* as the Common wretches that crawl on the earth.' Such teaching might lead to 'Disrespect towards Superiors'. Exaggerated stories were told, and it is unfortunate that so little of the anti-Methodist literature has any relationship to sense. Wesley himself is charged with being a Jacobite, the Pretender in disguise, a Jesuit, and a Quaker, of trying to betray England or the Church of England, of encouraging prostitution, and constantly of trying to make a huge fortune and of being a hypocrite. People believing some of these stories were easily inflamed by drunken squires and fox-hunting parsons to assail preachers with bricks and clubs. Many early preachers were badly hurt and one at least was killed.

The rich Lady Huntingdon adopted Whitefield and called in her fashionable friends to hear him. Her followers were strongly Calvinistic and insisted on their own views, but the Wesleys held different opinions, and the driving force of their message was Arminian, that *all* men might be saved.[1] The Whitefield section would neither compromise, nor leave the controversial point alone, and thus the movement was split. The Calvinistic Methodists[2] and Lady Huntingdon's Connexion still exist, but their numbers are small. For the first twenty years, however, it was the Whitefield branch that had the limelight, the vast crowds, the following in high life, and the bitter attacks in journals, in pamphlets, and on the stage. The Wesley side was better organized, quieter and more surely founded, and his societies persisted when the dramatic meetings were over. His preaching was much more ethical, more practical, simple and direct, and he had

[1] The best short account of this theological doctrine is in *Arminianism*, by A. W. Harrison, 1927. Briefly, it is defined there as 'the name given to the doctrines of Jacobus Arminius that were condemned at the Synod of Dort in 1619. His chief heresy consisted in his renunciation of the rigid Calvinistic decrees of predestination and reprobation. . . .' This protest had repercussions on politics and history as well as theology, and its ideas were carried over into many branches of thought.

A good account of the struggles between Calvinism and Arminianism, both in England and on the Continent, from 1600 to 1800 is found in the learned work of a Roman Catholic, Maximin Piette, *John Wesley in the Evolution of Protestantism*. This appeared in French in 1925, and there was an English translation in 1937.

[2] Now 'The Presbyterian Church of Wales'.

no tricks of oratory. Strangely enough, for a year or so in certain districts, it was at the preaching of Wesley that men dropped as dead, screamed and acted like madmen. He was worried at first, and never seems to have decided why these things happened, sometimes saying that the Devil attacked them, and sometimes that it was the hand of God. Some people simulated attacks, and when he left them severely alone soon recovered. The quietness and intensity of Wesley won him his converts. Numerous reports show that when a man heard Whitefield, he said, 'What an actor! What an orator! I think he is sincere'; but when he heard John Wesley he felt that he was alone with him and every word was addressed to him personally.

Charles Wesley had joined his brother in preaching and visiting the societies, and was even more shocked than his brother when he heard that certain unordained men had begun to preach. When John heard that Thomas Maxfield had begun to preach at the Foundery, he hurried there to stop him. His mother met him and, despite her High Church views, said: 'My son, I charge you before God, beware what you do; for Thomas Maxfield is as much called to preach the Gospel as ever you were.' He listened to him preaching, approved, and soon after had twenty travelling preachers. Many of these afterwards wrote their 'lives', which will be described later.

Wesley nowhere showed greater ability than in his choice of men. It was a hard life full of danger that he offered, with no chances of making money, and little of any settled home life. Each preaching house had a room for the visiting preacher to sleep in and a stable for his horse. Wesley insisted on wide reading and intensive study for some six or eight hours each day, and the travelling preachers were directly under his control and were sent where he chose. Few of the excesses attributed to the movement can have been committed by these men, so rigidly controlled, of obvious sincerity, and generally better instructed in theology and the Bible than the clergymen of the parishes they visited.[1]

[1] An account of the abilities and education of a large number of these travelling preachers is given in chap. vii.

The societies, in their turn, had their own leaders and some local preachers. Many of these were more un-educated men and may have given rise to some of the stories of the ignorance and superstition of Methodist preachers. Exaggeration has, however, played a large part, and it should be remembered that there were many little bogus societies which sprang up in imitation, and many cranks who went off to preach for a time. This ceased after a while, but the regularized Methodism persisted. The travelling preachers became the present Methodist Ministry and the local preachers are the present preaching Methodist laymen.

A very important point often overlooked is that the Methodists were members of the Church of England and had nothing whatever to do with Dissent. Ignorant writers who speak of eighteenth-century Dissent and Methodism as being one and the same thing wholly miss the point. The trouble was that Wesley persisted all his days in claiming his membership and trying to prove the rights of his case. No responsible bishop worried greatly about the habits of those peculiar people, Dissenters, but here were Church of England clergymen acting 'ugly enthusiasm'. The Methodist went to church on Sunday and was annoyingly regular: he took the Sacrament there and held no meeting during church hours. Some clergymen welcomed the movement and helped and attended the meeting house beside the church: more intolerant men drove them out and insulted them consistently. Though Wesley refused to see it, and till his death claimed to be a member of the Church of England, after his death a break became inevitable unless there could be some compromise. About 1750 he agreed to license his preaching houses because of insistent persecution, though he claimed there was no necessity for doing so, since they were not Dissenters; but his preachers objected to being imprisoned by intolerant magistrates for the sake of a phrase. A second stage in the break occurred when people who went to no church, as well as some Dissenters, joined his societies. They asked to be allowed to have their own services on Sundays during church hours. Wesley refused them for many years, but finally gave way where he found that the clergymen drove them from the church. The greatest legal break came after the American War of Independence, when there were no bishops and few clergy in America, and the English Church would send no one to administer the Sacraments. Wesley, who could have but little right to do so, though he produced many old arguments to justify himself, ordained men himself and sent them. The real justification was the need of the people. Later he ordained some to work in Scotland, and finally in England. After his death the break became complete, and Methodists gradually ceased to attend their parish church, though their doctrines remained the same, the appointed services for the Sacraments were almost unchanged, and the Book of Common Prayer continued to be used by some for morning services. To a churchman, the Methodist of the eighteenth century was merely a troublesome member of the Church of England, insisting that he was within his rights in attending Wesley's preaching house as well as his parish church.

It is no purpose of this book to trace in detail the history of the growth of Methodism during the century, though much is shown incidentally in the sections on the *Journal* and the *Letters*. From the large centres of London, Bristol, and Newcastle, smaller societies arose, and Wesley, who had absolute control, travelled continuously around them for fifty years. He stopped to preach wherever he could, but he had a regular plan and time-table for his movements. As he appointed travelling preachers to help him, he made a plan for their services and meetings, and placed them in whatever parts of the country he thought best. Later he gathered his preachers together once each year and had a conference with them. At this the preachers were stationed for the year, and after his death it became the supreme court and directory of Methodism. Even to-day, Methodist ministers are appointed at Conference to circuits, where they usually remain for three years. The 'room' for the preacher is to-day a furnished house, but the Methodist minister still remains a life-long traveller. When preachers married—and before marriage they were expected to consult Wesley on the suitability of the match—trouble arose over the education of their children. Wesley then built a school near Bristol, where the sons of the preachers and others could be boarded. This had classes of university standard, and Wesley sent some preachers there for training.

His own activities were far greater than preaching and organizing his society, for he had a vast correspondence and was frequently writing pamphlets and letters to papers and magazines in defence of the Methodist movement or his interpretation of doctrines. In addition, he founded a publishing house, re-issued classics and poetry and wrote educational books. From 1778 he ran a monthly magazine, the *Arminian Magazine*, in opposition to the Calvinistic *Gospel Magazine*. The large distribution of tracts and pamphlets, the sale of books at the Methodist centres, and the numerous educational publications had a considerable effect on both the movement and the country. The meeting houses became the centres of the life of the Methodists; from them they drew their instruction, and in them they discussed their problems, learned to express themselves clearly, and encouraged each other in thrift and ethical conduct. They tended to prosper in their business dealings, and towards the end of his life Wesley was bothered with the problem of rich Methodists.

A most important factor, too, was the stress on singing. Charles Wesley's gift of writing religious lyrical poetry was employed to the full, and popular tunes were found. The Methodists sang at all their meetings, and their hymn-books became their liturgy. The opportunities for discussion, for speaking in public, and especially for singing opened up a means of self-expression for masses of people, who found their recreation during the week at Methodist meeting houses. Possibly it tended to narrow their interests and, especially in the following century, they often became cut off from the entertainments of their neighbours. On the other hand, in country districts entertainments were crude and few, often consisting for the lower class in getting drunk. The Methodists became Puritans in their attitude towards entertainments, increasing in their strictness as time went on, but they kept their love of music, of singing, of religious poetry, and of educational books, and their meeting houses remained the centre of their social life. Thus, at the end of the eighteenth century, they formed a conservative, strongly ethical, and orderly mass of people who did much to prevent the spread of wilder and more emotional revolutionary ideas. Lecky has suggested that the Methodists prevented the French Revolution from spreading to England.

The Wesleys had separated from the Calvinistic section led by Whitefield and Lady Huntingdon soon after they began their work; nevertheless, John Wesley was always prepared to work with them or to allow Calvinists to preach for him. The opposing party was not nearly so accommodating, and kept up a running controversy and attack on the Arminians. When driven to reply, John Wesley wrote coldly ironical accounts of his opponents' opinions, and Charles Wesley, with less restraint, poured forth satirical verse. After six students had been expelled from Oxford on account of their 'enthusiasm' and Methodism, Lady Huntingdon, whose followers they were, set up a college at Trevecca to train young men in Calvinistic religion. John Wesley had remained on friendly terms with her, though he was always a little reserved and inclined to be critical of 'My Lady's Preachers'.

The wealth and high social standing of Lady Huntingdon[1] had established fashionable chapels, at Bath and Brighton and Tunbridge Wells, which were attended by many of the aristocracy. Records show that at times most of the distinguished people of her day visited her services, as, for example, Chesterfield, Horace Walpole, the Duchess of Argyll, Lady Betty Campbell, Lady Ferrars, Bubb Dodington, George Selwyn, Lord Holderness, the Duchess of Montagu, Lady Cardigan, Charles Townshend, Pitt, Lord North, Lord March, Lord Sandwich, and a multitude of others. Magnificent funerals were held for the Earl and Countess of

---

[1] The fullest account of Lady Huntingdon and of the fashionable side of Methodism is contained in *The Life and Times of Selina, Countess of Huntingdon*, two vols., 1840, by 'A Member of the Houses of Shirley and Hastings'. This is a most detailed account and contains a great number of letters from distinguished people.

Sutherland, and for the Earl of Buchan, and so great was the crowd that special tickets of admittance were issued. Great crowds came also to hear 'Mr. Whitefield improve upon the awful providence' when Lady Essex and Mrs. Charles Yorke 'died rather suddenly of sore throats'. It is difficult to estimate what influence this aristocratic Calvinistic preaching had on society, and though the majority came to observe and listen to the oratory, some of them were probably sincere in their support. For example, Lord Dartmouth, the Secretary for the Colonies with Lord North, was a genuine convert, and was praised by Cowper as 'One who wears a coronet and prays'. Lady Huntingdon was sincere as well as eccentric, and received the support of George III at Court. 'I wish there was a Lady Huntingdon in every diocese of the kingdom', he said. The fact, however, remains that the aristocratic section was the mere gaudy fringe of the movement, and to-day it is only of interest as showing that some forms of 'Methodism' touched all classes of English life.

On March 2, 1791, John Wesley died at his house in City Road, leaving the Methodist movement firmly established throughout the British Isles, America, and Canada. He remained within the Church of England all his life, though in his last years he realized that there must ultimately be a separation. There is little need to write of the character of John Wesley, for it is so clearly seen in all his works. Many have written critically and with hostility of the Methodist movement, but practically all are impressed by the greatness of its founder. Southey thought he saw Wesley's chief flaw in his ambition, but he afterwards changed his mind. With the letters of Wesley now available, this charge will not be repeated. He can be attacked for his autocracy, but it is difficult to imagine what might have happened to the movement had there not been some one capable of disciplining it and of keeping rigid control. Writers to-day criticize most often the superstitious and credulous side of his character, which was one of his most marked traits, though it is possibly ironic that this should be stressed in the present age with its belief in newspapers, new religions, legends of national heroes, and with the reappearance of astrologers. John

Wesley's credulity has been well described by Professor Elton:[1]

> Wesley's attitude towards the reasoning faculty deserves attention. At first we tax him with boundless credulity. In every incident, great or small, that turned out well, he saw, like Bunyan, a special providence. Much has been made of his proneness to accept a supernatural explanation at every turn. Tales of miraculous cures, of telepathy, and of sudden judgements upon blasphemers, he rarely sifts and usually believes. He was often pelted with stones, which he calls, in his nervous style, 'artillery, ready at hand, for the devil's drunken companions'. Sometimes they not only missed him but, by a peculiar mercy, hit some of his assailants who were pressing him hard. Black and white agents, unseen, are at work everywhere. Once his horse runs away with him and his two grand-children, and, on the edge of a precipice, stops short; and he gives seven reasons for thinking that 'both good and evil angels had a large share in this transaction'. . . .
> On this side of his mind Wesley belonged to the pre-critical age, and was at one with his audiences.
> None the less, Wesley is in his own way a spokesman of the 'age of reason'. He is prepared to argue for the truth of his stories; and he is on his mettle all the while to show that his cause is rational. . . .
> And he is ready to prove his case from Scripture as well as from 'experience'. He refuses to be called a 'mystic' and has all his life to fight against the word 'enthusiast'. It is best 'to drop the quietists and mystics altogether and at all hazards keep to the plain, practical, written word of God'.

Wesley's literary powers and influence on literature remain to be discussed later, and his remarkable knowledge of men and power of organization will be seen in the quotations from his works. Robert Southey, in his *Life of Wesley*, was bitter only when he saw Methodism as a separation from the Church of England, and ends his book by saying:

> Such was the life, and such the labours of John Wesley; a man of great views, great energy, and great virtues . . . who should be ranked not only among the most remarkable and influential men of his age, but among the great benefactors of his country and his kind.

[1] *A Survey of English Literature*, 1730–80, Oliver Elton, vol. ii, pp. 219–20.

THE JOURNAL OF JOHN WESLEY

The diary and the journal. Illustrations of Wesley's style from his accounts of travel, foreign countries, cathedrals, museums, journeys by horse, coach, and ship. The variety of his interests. Mob scenes. Old age. Other eighteenth-century journals and diaries. Merits of Wesley's *Journal*.

(All references to the *Journal* are taken from *The Journal of the Rev. John Wesley, A.M.* Edited by Nehemiah Curnock. Standard Edition. Eight vols. 1909.)

CHAPTER I

THE JOURNAL OF JOHN WESLEY[1]

Wesley's Journal has all the charm of a pious Pepys. . . . In pathos and descriptive power, its simple narrative shows the rugged force of Walt Whitman; the word is not sought for, it comes naturally, and, one feels, is inevitable. It is full of humour and observant to the very minutest detail of everything that concerns the daily life of mankind.

He gives to his everyday life, in all its realism, a touch of romance which shines through the stupendous record of what he did and said. . . . If we judge the Journal with the life which it lays bare, it is one of the great books of the world.[2]

THE *Journal* of John Wesley is his best-known work and has

---

[1] To make clear the difference between the diary and the journal, which are sometimes muddled by casual writers, a few facts must be remembered.

John Wesley began a diary on April 5, 1725, and continued it till his death. This varies in its details at different times, but generally consists of a short summary of his activities for every hour of the day. Often it contains a list of books he read and of people he met. It is composed of short phrases or single words, and from it he wrote his journals. The diary, which still exists in manuscripts, now in different parts of the world, was written in abbreviated longhand sometimes, in a special and varying kind of cipher at others, in Byrom's shorthand at other times, and on occasions in a mixture of these. The manuscripts between 1741 and 1790 are lost, but details from the other manuscripts were deciphered and incorporated in the Standard Edition of the *Journal*, published in 1909.

Wesley began his journal when he went to America, and sent it in manuscript to be read by his friends. There are many versions of portions of this still in existence—for example, five versions of the Georgia Journal exist, each copy with slight variations in detail and probably meant for different readers or improved with more revision. Wesley continually revised parts of his journal throughout his life.

When he returned from Georgia, there were many wild stories current about his behaviour there, so, in order to give an accurate account, he decided to publish some extracts from his journal, which was being read in manuscript by his friends. Accordingly in 1739 he published at Bristol, *An Extract of the Rev. Mr. John Wesley's Journal from his Embarking for Georgia to his Return to London*. Twenty more times during his life he published other extracts, the last day described being October 24, 1790.

[2] W. H. Hutton, in *The Cambridge History of English Literature*, vol. x, p. 36.

deservedly met with admiration from recent critics of English literature.[1] It is, perhaps, even better known to social historians, covering as it does so many phases of English life between 1735 and 1790:

> Here the history of society in the eighteenth century becomes pregnant with life, and certain of its most important phases, such as the growth of industrialism, and the development of the artisan classes, are made clearer. But there is more by way of revelation. All the psychology of religious revival, the influences contributing to its preparation, and scenes of conversion, the contagious power of its influence over whole masses of people, the spiritual anxiety and nervous unrest it gave rise to, the numerous individual backslidings, briefly the whole drama of the struggle between grace and human shortcomings, is here enacted before our eyes.[2]

Much of its interest lies in the picture it gives of every part of the British Isles, and its glimpses of life in America, Holland, and Germany. Many of the famous men of the day appear or are discussed in its pages, side by side with obscure men and women who came to Wesley for both spiritual and bodily advice. Not the least interesting portions are those accounts, sent to him by friends, of curious and unexplained happenings in Nature, or of strange illnesses and their cures. Side by side with dispassionate descriptions of riots and prisons and executions are notes on the various books Wesley read on his journeys, and, as Lecky has observed, 'One of the charms of the Journals is the large amount of shrewd literary criticism they contain'.[3]

While the fact remains that much of the fascination of the journals lies in the mixture of the contents, the outstanding feature is the account of one man's astonishing vigour and calm ability.

In order to give a short account of the varied contents of the *Journal*, I shall group Wesley's activities and interests together, looking first at the descriptions of his various methods of travel and of some of the places he visited.

[1] 'There is no printed English diary which in point of view of length and regularity can surpass the diaries and journals kept by John Wesley. . . . As a personal record of a life, it is the most voluminous that has been published.' Lord Ponsonby in *English Diaries*, p. 155.

[2] *A History of English Literature*, Louis Cazamian, p. 955.

[3] *England in the Eighteenth Century*, W. E. H. Lecky, vol. iii, p. 120.

The book opens with his journey to Georgia in 1735.[1] Leaving Gravesend on October 14, 1735, he travelled on the *Simmonds* and arrived in Georgia on February 6, 1736. The description of this voyage has been often quoted, but it is worth recalling:

Sunday, 25.

At noon our third storm began. At four it was more violent than any we had had before. . . . The winds roared round about us, and —what I never heard before—whistled as distinctly as if it had been a human voice. The ship not only rocked to and fro with the utmost violence, but shook and jarred with so unequal, grating a motion, that one could not but with great difficulty keep one's hold of any-thing, nor stand a moment without it. Every ten minutes came a shock against the stern or side of the ship, which one would think should dash the planks in a thousand pieces. . . .

At seven I went to the Germans. I had long before observed the great seriousness of their behaviour. . . . In the midst of the psalm wherewith their service began, the sea broke over, split the main-sail in pieces, covered the ship, and poured in between the decks, as if the great deep had already swallowed us up. A terrible scream-ing began among the English. The Germans looked up, and with-out intermission calmly sang on. I asked one of them afterwards, 'Was you not afraid?' He answered, 'I thank God, no'. I asked, 'But were not your women and children afraid?' He replied mildly, 'No; our women and children are not afraid to die'.

From them I went to their crying, trembling neighbours. . . . At twelve the wind fell. . . .[2]

Wesley made forty-two visits to Ireland and frequently noted the difficulty in securing a boat. He said that there were three rules that should be learned by those who desired to make this crossing. They were:

1. Never pay till you set sail.
2. Go not on board till the captain goes on board.
3. Send not your baggage on board till you go yourself.[3]

---

[1] Another diarist of the time was deeply interested in Oglethorpe's 'Georgia Society of Colonization'. In 1730 the Earl of Egmont began his diary, the first part of which has been published as *Manuscripts of the Earl of Egmont. Diary of Viscount Perceval, afterwards first Earl of Egmont* (Historical Manu-scripts Commission, 1920).

He was a strong Protestant and gave several descriptions of the meetings of the Georgia Society.

He has another faint connexion with Wesley; for in 1732 he noted that he 'dined with Dr. Delany and his lady'.

[2] *Journal*, vol. i, pp. 141–6. [3] *Ibid.*, vol. iv, p. 280.

He liked the Irish, finding them generous and hospitable, and said, 'Indeed, so civil a people in general I never saw, either in Europe or America'.[1]

His visits to Scotland were fewer than those to Ireland, and Edinburgh is called 'one of the dirtiest cities I had ever seen, not excepting Cologne in Germany'.[2] On another occasion he described Holyrood Palace, and seized the opportunity once again to defend Mary Queen of Scots, whose cause he always upheld against Queen Elizabeth. He found the Spey 'the most impetuous river I ever saw', and at Aberbrothwick Abbey was infuriated by the sight of the ruins. 'The zealous Reformers, they told us, burnt this down. God deliver us from reforming mobs!'[3]

It would be easy to enumerate the various towns he visited and to quote his pithy descriptions of the inhabitants. He went to Shakespeare's Cliff at Dover to compare it with the description in *King Lear*, and found it 'nothing so terrible in itself as it is in his description'; at the age of seventy-seven he climbed Boston Steeple, 'which I suppose is by far the highest tower in the Kingdom'; and at the age of eighty-two he went to Land's End 'in order to which we clambered down the rocks, to the very edge of the water; and I cannot think but the sea has gained some hundred yards since I was here forty years ago'.[4]

Of the foreign countries that he visited, Holland pleased him the most. In 1739 he visited Amsterdam:

[1] *Journal*, vol. iii, p. 340.

[2] *Ibid.*, vol. iii, p. 523. Cologne seems to have struck many travellers by its dirt and smells. Coleridge in 1834 referred to 'the body-and-soul-stinking town of Cologne' in a poem, 'On My Joyful Departure'. In another poem, 'Cologne', he said:

> In Köln, a town of monks and bones,
> And pavements fang'd with murderous stones
> And rags, and hags, and hideous wenches;
> I counted two-and-seventy stenches,
> All well defined, and several stinks!
> Ye nymphs that reign o'er sewers and sinks,
> The river Rhine, it is well known,
> Doth wash your city of Cologne;
> But tell me, nymphs! what power divine
> Shall henceforth wash the river Rhine?

The Poems of S. T. Coleridge, Oxford Edition, p. 477.

[3] *Ibid.*, vol. v, p. 366.   [4] *Ibid.*, vol. vii, p. 109.

The exact neatness of all the buildings here, the nice cleanness of the streets (which, we were informed, were all washed twice a week), and the canals which run through all the main streets, with rows of trees on either side, make this the pleasantest city which I have ever seen.[1]

In common with his contemporaries, he took an enormous interest in great houses and their gardens. As he grew older he frequently turned out of his way to visit and give an account of some of these. For an example from the many he described, here is that of the Leasowes, which belonged to the poet Shenstone:

I went to Leasowes, a farm so called, four or five miles from Hagley. I never was so surprised. I have seen nothing in all England to be compared with it. It is beautiful and elegant all over. There is nothing grand, nothing costly; no temples, so called; no statues (except two or three, which had better have been spared); but such walks, such shades, such hills and dales, such lawns, such artless cascades, such waving woods, with water intermixed, as exceeded all imagination! On the upper side, from the openings of a shady walk is a most beautiful and extensive prospect. And all this is comprised in the compass of three miles! I doubt if it be exceeded by anything in Europe.[2]

He took friends to see several cathedrals, and to admire the monument to Admiral Tyrell in Westminster Abbey which was greatly praised in the eighteenth century and called 'the nadir of degradation in art' in the nineteenth.[3]

In 1738 he saw Cologne Cathedral and wrote:

We went to the Cathedral, which is mere heaps upon heaps; a huge misshapen thing, which has no more of symmetry than of neatness belonging to it.

This would seem to join him with Smollett, who complained of the propriety and proportion of York Minster, and in *Humphry Clinker* described Durham Cathedral as a 'huge,

[1] *Journal*, vol. ii, p. 5.   [2] *Ibid.*, vol. vi, p. 361.

[3] Archdeacon Farrar. See Note to *Journal*, vol. v, p. 401. It is interesting to see how taste varies from age to age. In an article on 'Sculpture', Katherine A. Eadaile has said of Wesley's view: 'If we are to be fair to the sculpture of Johnson's age, it is Wesley's verdict not Ruskin's or Dean Stanley's that we must accept' (*Johnson's England*, Ed. A. S. Turberville, 1933, vol. ii, p. 84).

gloomy pile'.[1] It would be a false comparison, however, for Wesley described Beverley Minster as 'a most beautiful as well as stately building', and greatly admired York and Lincoln Cathedrals. It has recently been pointed out that his account of Cologne Cathedral was accurate in 1738, when it was only half its present height and had a squat roof. The spires were added much later and the present building only completed in 1880.[2]

In the *Journal* are descriptions of the Physic Gardens in Chelsea and of numerous museums and waxworks. He spent some afternoons at the British Museum examining the exhibits from Ohteheite, and said Cox's Museum was full of 'pretty, glittering trifles', though he was much more interested in Spring Gardens:

I was desired to see the celebrated wax-works at the Museum in Spring Gardens. It exhibits most of the crowned heads in Europe, and shows their characters in their countenance. Sense and majesty appear in the King of Spain; dullness and sottishness in the King of France; infernal subtlety in the King of Prussia (as well as in the skeleton Voltaire); calmness and humanity in the Emperor and King of Portugal; exquisite stupidity in the Prince of Orange; and amazing coarseness, with everything that is unamiable in the Czarina.[3]

In 1786, he went to hear George III deliver his speech in the House of Lords. 'How agreeably was I surprised! He pronounced every word with exact propriety. I much doubt whether there be any other King in Europe that is so just and natural a speaker.'[4] When he visited the House of Lords on another occasion, he was not so favourably impressed, and he wrote:

I spent two or three hours in the House of Lords. I had frequently heard that this was the most venerable assembly in England. But how was I disappointed! What is a lord but a sinner, born to die.[5]

---

[1] *Humphry Clinker*, World's Classics Edition, p. 246. Matthew Bramble is writing, so this need not of necessity represent Smollett's views. Other characters, however, give similar views about the cathedrals and churches seen on their journey.

[2] For information about Cologne Cathedral I am indebted to *Studies in Literature*, by Henry Bett, 1929.

[3] *Journal*, vol. vii, p. 347.   [4] *Ibid.*, vol. vii, p. 136.

[5] *Ibid.*, vol. vii, p. 46.

Of his journeys, amounting to 3,000 miles a year, we do not hear enough. He states that he rode to certain places, preached on a certain text, was drenched in a storm, was lost on the moors, or was wetted through when crossing a ford, almost with indifference. His saddle-bags were filled with books which he read as he rode along in good weather. Only a few times was he thrown head over heels. He thus describes his method:

In this journey as well as in many others, I observed a mistake that almost universally prevails; and I desire all travellers to take good notice of it, which may save them both from trouble and danger. Near thirty years ago I was thinking, 'How is it that no horse ever stumbles while I am reading?' (History, poetry, and philosophy I commonly read on horseback, having other employment at other times.) No account can possibly be given but this: because then I throw the reins on his neck. I then set myself to observe; and I aver that, in riding above a hundred thousand miles, I scarce ever remember any horse (except two, that would fall head over heels anyway) to fall, or make a considerable stumble, while I rode *with* a *slack rein*. To fancy, therefore, that a tight rein prevents stumbling is a capital blunder. I have repeated the trial more frequently than most men in the kingdom can do. A slack rein will prevent stumbling, if anything will. But in some horses nothing can.[1]

One of the commands that he gave all his preachers, was: 'Be merciful to your beast. Not only ride moderately, but see with your own eyes that your horse be rubbed, fed, and bedded.'[2] As he grew old, he was forced to travel by coach, and there are short accounts of him talking to other occupants, or discussing the highwaymen that he never met, or annotating his 'Shakespeare'. Sometimes there are more graphic pictures:

I took coach for London. I was nobly attended; behind the coach were ten convicted felons, loudly blaspheming and rattling their chains; by my side sat a man with a loaded blunderbuss and another upon the coach.[3]

At Hull on another occasion the mob stoned him in a crowded coach, 'but a large gentlewoman, who sat in my lap, screened me, so that nothing came near me'.[4]

[1] *Journal*, vol. v, p. 361.   [2] *Works*, vol. viii, p. 317.
[3] *Journal*, vol. vi, p. 246.   [4] *Ibid.*, vol. iv, p. 21.

Of his own personal dangers he is very reticent, and it is from other sources that we learn of the real atrocities of the mobs. His descriptions of some of these scenes might have been written by a detached observer, and are remarkable for their understatement and ironic humour. He seems to have had no personal fears whatever. When describing a howling mob outside a house in which he was staying, he wrote:

When I had done preaching, I would have gone out to them, it being my rule, confirmed by long experience, always to look a mob in the face; but our people took me up whether I would or no, and carried me into the house.[1]

Professor Elton has laid stress on Wesley's humane temper, his love for children, and his care for animals.[2] He quotes for an example the incident when drunken opponents, who wished to break up an open-air meeting, drove a bull into the crowd:

When they had forced their way to the little table on which I stood, they strove several times to throw it down, by thrusting the helpless beast against it; who of himself, stirred no more than a log of wood. I once or twice put aside his head with my hand, that the blood might not drop upon my clothes.[3]

The worst riots were in Staffordshire, and on one occasion Wesley with some of his followers was driven into a house while the crowd began to smash in the windows and doors. The leader of the mob, however, was pushed inside, and to his horror was forced to share the danger with Wesley:

He did not like this, and would fain have got out; but it was not possible, so he kept as close to me as he could, thinking himself safe when he was near me: but, staying a little behind—when I went up two pairs of stairs, and stood close on one side where we were a little sheltered—a large stone struck him on the forehead, and the blood spouted out like a stream. He cried out, 'Oh, sir, are we to die to-night? What must I do? What must I do?' I said, 'Pray to God. He is able to deliver you from all danger'. He took my advice and began praying in such a manner as he had scarce done since he was

1 *Journal*, vol. iii, p. 250.
2 *A Survey of English Literature, 1730–80*, Oliver Elton, vol. ii, p. 215.
3 *Journal*, vol. ii, p. 534.

born. . . . They filled the house at once, and proposed setting it on fire; but one of them, happening to remember that his own house was next, with much ado persuaded them not to do it.[1]

The most lengthy description of riotous scenes is another in Staffordshire when two mobs carried him off:

> I went into the midst and brought the head of the mob with me up to the desk. I received but one blow on the side of the head; after which we reasoned the case till he grew milder.

An account of being dragged through the streets follows:

> Till a little before ten God brought me safe to Wednesbury, having lost only one flap of my waistcoat and a little skin from one of my hands. . . . From the beginning to the end I found the same presence of mind as if I had been sitting in my own study. But I took no thought for one moment before another; only once it came into my mind that, if they should throw me into the river, it would spoil the papers that were in my pocket. For myself, I did not doubt that I should swim across, having but a thin coat and a light pair of boots.[2]

Charles Wesley met him when he was coming away from Staffordshire and wrote: 'He looked like a soldier of Christ; his clothes were torn to tatters; but his work is not finished.' Passing over other accounts of his adventures with mobs and the difficulties he endured by road and by sea, I shall quote a few more trivial incidents.

Charles Lamb ascribed the charm of Cowper's letters to their 'divine chit-chat', and it is partly Wesley's lapses from high seriousness that make his *Journal* so readable. Generally he holds his humour severely in check, fearing that levity may hinder him, but his sense of irony continually breaks through in small incidents. For examples, here are two short episodes:

> One came to me, as she said, with a message from the Lord, to tell me I was laying up treasures on earth, taking my ease, and minding only my eating and drinking. I told her, God knew me better; and, if He had sent her, He would have sent her with a more proper message.[3]

---

[1] *Journal*, vol. iii, p. 331. [2] *Ibid.*, vol. iii, pp. 93, 100–3.
[3] *Ibid.*, vol. iv, p. 364.

I buried the remains of poor E. T., of whom *ever since she died* her husband speaks as a most excellent woman, and a most affectionate wife.[1]

He was filled with almost insatiable curiosity which seems to have grown stronger as he grew older. He stopped near Northampton to measure 'the largest elm I ever saw; it was twenty-eight feet in circumference, six feet more than that which was some years ago in Magdalen College walks at Oxford'.[2]

He paused at Sevenoaks to remark: 'In the year 1769, I weighed a hundred and twenty-two pounds. In 1783 I weighed not a pound more or less.'[3] He described having his portrait painted twice in 1787: of the first: 'I think it is the best that ever was taken; but what is the picture of a man above four score?'; of the second: 'At the earnest desire of Mrs. Tighe, I once more sat for my picture. Mr. Romney is a painter indeed. He struck off an exact likeness at once; and did more in one hour than Sir Joshua did in ten.'[4] The Reynolds picture painted in 1755 is now lost.

It is not my intention here to discuss his views on art and architecture, but merely to give a short description of the variety of his *Journal*. But from the quotations given, it can be seen that his taste was typical of his own time. The statues and monuments which he admired most were those of contemporary artists, and though he had a strong liking for Gothic architecture his own ideals were those of Wren. The meeting houses and preachers' houses erected by him, as, for example, those beautifully restored in Bristol and in City Road, London, are typical examples of eighteenth-century work, plain, dignified, and designed for utility. He showed, too, the contemporary liking for scientific collections in museums and gardens, and the love of landscape gardening. He has no descriptions of mountains in England or Germany, but goes into detail about Holland. Though much more will be said about his views and tastes in later chapters, they might well be summarized as those of a gentleman of his own time.

[1] *Journal*, vol. v, p. 497. [2] *Ibid.*, vol. vi, p. 4.
[3] *Ibid.*, vol. vi, p. 462.. [4] *Ibid.*, vol. vii, p. 461.

A curious account is given of an experiment with the lions in the Tower:

I thought it would be worth while to make an odd experiment. Remembering how surprisingly fond of music the lion at Edinburgh was, I determined to try whether this was the case with all animals of the same kind. I accordingly went to the Tower with one who plays on the German flute. He began playing near four or five lions; only one of these (the rest not seeming to regard it at all) rose up, came to the front of his den, and seemed to be all attention. Meantime a tiger in the same den started up, leaped over the lion's back, turned and ran under his belly, leaped over him again, and so to and fro incessantly. Can we account for this by any principle of mechanism? Can we account for it at all?[1]

Some ten years later, at Sir Ashton Lever's museum, he was fascinated with the stuffed animals. 'The hippopotamus, in particular, looks as fierce as if he was just coming out of the river; and the old lion appears as formidable now as when he was stalking in the Tower.'[2] Only a few months before he died, when he could only write with great difficulty, he described a monster he had been to see, and gave an account of a pelican.

Towards the close of his life he described his health every year. On his eighty-fifth birthday he noted that he could remember the people and events of his youth better than more recent happenings, but remarked that he had little other trouble. Among the causes of his good health were:

(2) To my never having lost a night's sleep, sick or well, at land or at sea, since I was born.
(3) To my having sleep at command, so that whenever I feel myself almost worn out I call it, and it comes, day or night. . . .
(6) To my having had so little pain in my life, or so little sorrow or anxious care.[3]

At eighty-six, he wrote, 'I now find I grow old', and on October 24, 1790, he ceased to write his journal, but he managed to continue with his diary till his death on March 2, 1791.

I have purposely avoided quoting from the *Journal*

[1] *Journal*, vol. v, p. 104.   [2] *Ibid.*, vol. vi, p. 267.
[3] *Ibid.*, vol. vii, p. 408. Southey shows his antipathy to Wesley when he remarks about Wesley's ability to sleep at any time, 'Like a mere animal'.

extracts that deal with Wesley's own work and the formation of the Methodist societies, because unsympathetic writers about the *Journal* have sometimes suggested that it consisted of theological writing interspersed with stories of doubtful veracity or which showed Wesley's credulous nature. It is, of course, true that a great part of the *Journal* is concerned with Wesley's own labours, his preaching at different towns, his interviews with converts and critics, and his actions and opinions concerning the political and social happenings around him; but I have tried to show that all this is enlivened with a great variety of other matter. The large amount of literary criticism, the accounts of the books he read and the famous people he met are treated in detail in later chapters of this study, and are mentioned only now to stress other aspects of the *Journal*. A complete reading of the whole *Journal* leaves two strong impressions: first, of the vigour and energy of Wesley, and, second, of his wide interests and variety of tastes.

This is brought home more clearly when his *Journal* is compared with some similar journals and diaries of his own time.[1]

George Whitefield's journals[2] and *Accounts* of his own life are chiefly concerned with his own journeys and his own progress and ability in spreading the Gospel. The reader tends to feel that, despite the interesting asides, the writer is always explaining his own actions. His journal is his apology. Wesley's *Journal* is something far wider in scope than this.

The journal of Charles Wesley was not published in his lifetime and possibly was written for circulation among a select group of friends. Occasionally he is more outspoken about individual people or more satirical about events than

---

[1] See *English Diaries*, by Arthur Ponsonby, M.P. This has a most interesting account of many eighteenth-century diaries, but the section on John Wesley is not good. There are a number of inaccuracies: 'he was practically always well in health'; he was converted listening to a sermon; 'best of all he loved preaching in open fields': he preached with *excited* eloquence; he was 'no lover of quiet days'; his reading was mainly theological; his imperious ambition, etc. Lord Ponsonby stresses the *Journal* chiefly as a sermon record, and fails to find Wesley human. 'The pedestal is too high, we cannot reach him, and it is extraordinarily tiring even to attempt to follow him in his interminable journeys and his unending sermons.'

[2] See chap. viii.

his brother, whose *Journal* could be read by all, but Charles's audience was expected to be chiefly interested in his religious changes and emotions and in detailed accounts of his known actions. He wrote it so that a select band of his contemporaries could read it, and he meant it to make a certain impression on them.[1]

In marked contrast to this was *The Private Journal of John Byrom*, which was never intended for publication. He wrote this in his own system of shorthand as a kind of memoranda from day to day, and it consists simply of an account of his own actions during the course of each day, with no excuses or self-praise, and with nothing put in to impress other readers. This is now its charm; but he had few indiscretions in his somewhat uneventful life, and though his *Journal*[2] is of interest, it is doubtful if it will ever be widely read.

John Wesley followed Byrom closely in one respect; he used his system of shorthand to keep his diary—when he did not use a private cipher of his own. This diary containing brief notes of what he did from hour to hour was intended only for his own use, as a record of events and time spent, as rough materials for his *Journal*, and to register his religious feelings. Thus, the diary in its aim was probably similar to that of Byrom, though completely unlike it in form.

Little purpose would be served in continuing a comparison of Wesley's *Journal* with those more famous journals of other ages, but a completely dissimilar contemporary one must be mentioned, *The Diary of a Country Parson*. Few clerical lives can have been in greater contrast to that of John Wesley than the Rev. James Woodforde's in the quiet villages of Somerset and Norfolk. He lived his life in seclusion, enjoying the homely events around him and noting the nature of his meals. He was practically untouched by the politics or social events of his time, though he twice mentions Methodism.

A note on 'Brother John' says that there was a story that he 'once rode his favourite horse into a Methodist Chapel

[1] The journals of George Whitefield and Charles Wesley are described in chap. viii.
[2] *The Private Journal and Literary Remains of John Byrom*. Ed. R. Parkinson. Printed for the Chetham Society, 1855.

and cursed the congregation'. He sobered down before his death in 1799, and his wife survived him till 1826. 'She is said to have been a friend of Wesley's, and possibly that very great man influenced her husband in later life.'[1] This story may well have been true; for Wesley, in his *Journal* for September 27, 1787, says that all was then quiet at that village, Castle-Cary, whereas some years before a Methodist was flung into the horse-pond there.

Parson Woodforde's other reference to Methodists was on April 27, 1801, when he wrote:

We heard the Cuckoo for the first time. Dinner to-day, a pike roasted, etc. I still continue very weak and spiritless. A Methodist Meeting we heard to-day is held at Whisson's House on Sundays— very near us.[2]

The contents of the journals of Wesley and Woodforde are so widely different, although they are contemporary accounts of Church of England clergymen, that comparisons are futile.[3]

---

[1] *The Diary of a Country Parson*, by the Rev. James Woodforde, 1924, vol. i, p. 177.

[2] *Ibid.*, vol. v, p. 312.

[3] It is of interest to note that Wesley met another diarist of the time, the Quaker, Dr. Rutty. He records meeting him in Dublin on his second and third visits to Ireland in 1748 and 1749. On each occasion Dr. Rutty insisted on Wesley resting for a day or so. Dr. Rutty began his diary in 1753 and ended it in 1774. Wesley records meeting him again in 1775: 'I visited that venerable man, Dr. Rutty, just tottering over the grave; but still clear in his understanding, full of faith and love, and patiently waiting till his change should come' (*Journal*, vol. vi, p. 58). Dr. Rutty was an excellent man and treated many poor people and Methodist preachers without charging them. He kept his diary to encourage himself to live more virtuously. He fought a never-ending battle against his vices, over-eating, over-drinking, shortness of temper, and fondness for sleep. After his death, for the encouragement of others, his diary was published in London: *A Spiritual Diary and Soliloquies*, by John Rutty, M.D., late of Dublin. Two vols., 1777. There is one reference to Methodists. On April 13, 1757, he wrote: 'The Methodists hold conferences on spiritual experiences: I hitherto in a lower sphere, on meer body: thus the least in the Kingdom of heaven is greater than I.' The interest now lies in his truthful accounts of his struggles and failures, some examples of which are:

A feast—pretty sober . . . lived to drink: and the head-ache a most righteous consequence. . . . Drank to the utmost bounds, if not beyond. . . . Piggish at a feast. . . . A little swinish at dinner. . . . Eight in the morning: O the time lost in bed. . . . Snapped at a pauper. . . . Eight o'clock cold and sleepy. The King of Spain rises at five.

His last entry, on December 8, 1774, was: 'The voice of God now sounds louder in my great infirmity, of being scarcely able to bear the cold.'

The question then arises: why did Wesley write a journal? Were he to have given a reply himself he would doubtlessly have replied that he wrote and published these accounts of his life to save men's souls. He hoped they would read of the strange happenings in the land and of the great changes wrought on men's lives, and come to investigate for themselves. He thought that these straightforward accounts would dispel some of the strange rumours and exaggerated reports that were always rife, and he hoped that his own followers would find encouragement as they read. All this is probably true and supplies the first reasons for the publication of the *Journal* at different times.

It is not adequate, however, to explain the *Journal* as we find it. If the edification of mankind was the sole object, why was so much of the matter included at all? What ethical values are to be found in some of his literary criticisms, or in the descriptions of his measuring the girth of elm trees and testing the effect of music on lions? The descriptions of some of the country gardens, of the life in Georgia, of the storms at sea, and of many peculiar incidents on his travels are given with the skill of a novelist. Often his incidents are described with all the care and restraint of Swift, whose prose he most admired. At other times, in homely descriptions and in detail which gives a feeling of veracity, he closely follows Defoe. Whatever his reasons, or excuses, for publication, behind the *Journal* lies the artistic urge for expression which is behind all great writing. There is no moral reason why at least a quarter of the *Journal* should have been published, but this quarter has been written with great care both in choice of incident and of language. Much of the *Journal* was written because Wesley enjoyed writing it, and in this he might well be compared with Pepys.

It is not my intention to discuss here Wesley's character as seen in his *Journal*, nor to stress further that it is an account of English life as seen by a very observant English gentleman of the time. These facts will be made clear in succeeding chapters, where as often as possible I shall let Wesley speak for himself. Those who have read the *Journal* and the other works carefully have nearly always felt their charm and value, and for the end of this section I shall quote the words of Augustine Birrell:

> Let no one deny charm to Wesley who has not read his *Journal*. Southey's *Life* is a dull, almost a stupid, book, which happily there is no need to read. Read the *Journal*, which is a book full of plots and plays and novels, which quivers with life, and is crammed full of character. . . .
>
> Wesley remained all his life very much the scholar and the gentleman. . . . He was no alarmist, no sentimentalist; he never gushed, seldom exaggerated, and always wrote on an easy level. . . . Ride up and down with the greatest force of the eighteenth century in England.[1]

[1] *The Collected Essays and Addresses of the Right Hon. Augustine Birrell*, 1922, vol. i, p. 301.

THE LETTERS OF JOHN WESLEY

The nature of the Letters. Early Letters. Politics and Controversy.
Advice to preachers. Humour and brevity. Old age. Wesley as
a Letter-writer.

(All references are taken from *The Letters of the Rev. John Wesley,*
A.M. Edited John Telford. Standard Edition. Eight vols. 1931.)

CHAPTER II

THE LETTERS OF JOHN WESLEY

THOUGH many of the longer letters of John Wesley had been published in the *Collected Works*, it was not until 1931 that the complete edition was available. These eight volumes, with their exhaustive notes, fill in a great many of the blank spaces in the *Journal*, and illuminate many of the obscure episodes of Wesley's life. They give intimate pictures of Wesley at work and of the rise of Methodism, although even in his letters he was reticent about his own private sorrows and feelings.

The letters cover the years 1721 to 1791, and all the years are represented except 1722 and 1728. They are written to all classes of people in Great Britain and America and, besides dealing with the religious problems of individuals and giving commands and instructions to his preachers and followers, touch on all sides of life, literary criticism, education, religious and scientific controversy, social problems and politics.

There are 2,670 letters in this collection, which can only be a fraction of those he wrote. The great letter-writer of the time, Horace Walpole, has 3,060 letters in his collection, and his letters naturally show the larger amount of leisure that he enjoyed. The Wesley letters are clear, concise, and definite. The general impression gathered is of a man having certain important things to say, and saying them with directness and simplicity. There are, of course, exceptions, in his earlier years, in letters of controversy, and in the more intimate letters on religious subjects. The view of Wesley as a man rushing breathlessly from place to place, as a man fighting a continual General Election,[1] is erroneous. His

---

[1] *Selected Essays*, Augustine Birrell, 1922.

life was filled with a passion for orderly planning: everything was so planned that all things could be fitted in with ease. He believed that he had the largest correspondence of any man in Europe, and he made it a rule to reply to all. He explained his manner of finding time to Miss March in 1776:

> You do not at all understand my manner of life. Though I am always in haste, I am never in a hurry; because I never undertake any more work than I can go through with perfect calmness of spirit. It is true I travel four or five thousand miles in a year. But I generally travel alone in my carriage, and consequently am as retired ten hours in a day as if I was in a wilderness. On other days I never spend less than three hours (frequently ten or twelve) in the day alone.[1]

Sometimes, in order to write longer letters on controversial matters, he retired to a friend's house for a few days; but the majority were written while he was on the way.

The first letters are those written home to Epworth from Charterhouse and Oxford, and already begin to show his chief interests. He was always fascinated by medicine and cures for illness, reading books on the subject whenever he could spare time, and experimenting whenever he could get a chance. The cure given in the letter home to his mother in 1723 was reproduced in his later publication, *Primitive Physick, or an Easy and Natural Method of Curing Most Diseases*:

> I am very glad to hear that all at home are well; as I am, I thank God at present, being seldom troubled with anything but bleeding at the nose, which I have frequently. A little while ago, it bled so violently while I was walking in the evening a mile or two from Oxford, that it almost choked me; nor did any method I could use at all abate it, till I stripped myself and leapt into the river, which happened luckily not to be far off.[2]

This method of cure was starred in his later book as a remedy *Tried*. From Oxford he wrote to his brother Samuel: 'Leisure and I have taken leave of one another. I propose to be busy as long as I live.'[3]

An interesting set of letters resulted from the friendship of the Wesleys with the Granville family. Around 1730, John and his brother Charles frequently visited this family and

---

[1] *Letters*, vol. vi, p. 292.   [2] *Ibid.*, vol. i, p. 6.   [3] *Ibid.*, vol. i, p. 34.

began to correspond with them. For a time it looked as if John Wesley would propose marriage to Mrs. Pendarves, afterwards Mrs. Delany. A polite, semi-serious flirtation took place, and there were walks in gardens during which they discussed the state of their souls in terms befitting High Church gentility. These were the days before any one dreamed of mentioning 'enthusiasm' in connexion with the Wesleys. Long, artificial letters were written between members of this circle, the correspondents never signing their own names, but adopting pastoral terms. A considerable number remain, fanciful, charmingly polite epistles, with little requests for poems and hymns, decorous accounts of the health of their souls, and arrangements for further meetings. Charles Wesley had already begun to write hymns; for Selima wrote, 'Is not Araspes' hymn quite charming?'[1]

Reality returns when Wesley became a tutor at Oxford. Possibly reacting from his failure to woo satisfactorily, he flung himself with furious zeal into his new duties. His passion for order and thoroughness was applied to his teaching methods, and his pupils' lives were planned with the same rigour that he applied to himself. He planned out his work for every moment of the day and began his day at four in the morning. There follows an amusing set of letters, when a bright young man, Richard Morgan, arrived at Oxford 'with a greyhound' and found that his tutor was John Wesley. There are frantic letters home to father in Ireland protesting at the amount of work required by the tutor, exaggerating the 'orgies of piety' at the Holy Club and begging for a change to a less serious instructor. The father, however, had great faith in Wesley, and though he suggested a little more leniency, he had no word of comfort for his son. Describing the Wesleys and their friends, Richard Morgan wrote to his father:

[1] Many letters from other members of the group are given in footnotes of the Standard Edition of John Wesley's *Letters*. The most detailed account of the whole affair is in *Son to Susanna*, by G. E. Harrison, 1937, and in two books by E. C. Vulliamy, *John Wesley*, 1931, and *Aspasia: The Life and Letters of Mrs. Delany, 1700–1788*. Mrs. Delany's letters are fully given in *Autobiography and Correspondence of Mary Granville (Mrs. Delany)*, edited by the Right Hon. Lady Llanover, 1861.

They imagine they cannot be saved if they do not spend every hour, nay minute, of their lives in the service of God. . . . I have not been an hour idle since I came to College but when I walk for my health, which he himself advises. . . . In short, labouring under all these disadvantages, I am grown perfectly melancholy, and have got such an habit of sighing, which I cannot avoid, that it must certainly do me great mischief.[1]

The father's heartless reply was, 'Banish your dog immediately'. A few years later, the young man and Wesley were great friends and Morgan was one who came to see him off for America. It is a striking fact that throughout his life all Wesley's opponents who met him came to like him.

Leaving the letters of youth and those of the High Church period, I shall next consider those written about national affairs. The *Journal* and the *Letters* need to be read together for graphic accounts of the '45 Rebellion, when Wesley was at Newcastle expecting the rebels. Later he rode south and carried the news of their defeats. He was an ardent supporter of King George, though he was everywhere faced with accusations that he was a Jacobite. His passion for 'the best of Kings' was so great that when England was threatened with a French invasion in 1756, he wrote to James West, M.P., offering to raise and lead 200 volunteers. These would be—

supported by contributions among themselves; and to be ready in case of an invasion to act for a year (if needed so long) at His Majesty's pleasure. . . . If this be acceptable to His Majesty, they beg to have arms out of the Tower, giving the usual security for their return, and some of His Majesty's sergeants to instruct them in the military exercise.[2]

Years later, in the American crisis, Wesley was able to speak with knowledge and to prophesy with accuracy. At the beginning of the war he wrote to Charles Wesley: 'Just what I thought at first, I think still of American affairs. If a blow is struck, I give America for lost, and perhaps England too.'[3]

At the outbreak of the war he wrote to Lord North and to

[1] *Letters*, vol. i, pp. 147, 149.   [2] *Ibid.*, vol. iii, p. 165.
[3] *Ibid.*, vol. vi, p. 152.

the Earl of Dartmouth, the Secretary of State for the Colonies:

All my prejudices are against the Americans. For I am an High Churchman, the son of an High Churchman, bred up from my childhood in the highest notions of passive obedience and non-resistance. And yet, in spite of all my rooted prejudice, I cannot avoid thinking (if I think at all) that an oppressed people asked for nothing more than their legal rights, and that in the most modest and inoffensive way which the nature of the thing would allow. But waiving this, waiving all considerations of right and wrong, I ask, Is it common sense to use force toward the Americans? . . . Indeed some of our valiant officers say, 'Two thousand men will clear America of these rebels'. No, nor twenty thousand, nor perhaps treble that number, be they rebels or not. They are as strong men as you; they are as valiant as you, if not abundantly more valiant. For they are one and all enthusiasts—enthusiasts for liberty. They are calm, deliberate enthusiasts. . . . 'But they are divided among themselves': so you are informed by various letters and memorials. So, I doubt not, was poor Rehoboam informed concerning the ten tribes. . . . Have they not another considerable advantage? Is there occasion to recruit the troops? Their supplies are at hand, all round about them: ours are three thousand miles off.[1]

In conclusion, Wesley suggested that the French and Spaniards would join with the Americans.

As soon as the war had properly begun, Wesley's views of the rights and wrongs of the case were changed by reading Dr. Johnson's tract on the subject; but his publications and other actions during the struggle are dealt with in a later section.

Wesley is seen at his best when writing to his preachers and helpers to give them practical and homely advice and to offer them constructive criticism. He was constantly restraining them from excesses of any kind, exhorting them to avoid 'enthusiasm' and commanding them to read and study more. To John Downes he wrote, 'How are you employed?—from five in the morning till nine at night? For I suppose you want eight hours' sleep. What becomes of logic and Latin?'[2] Services conducted by his preachers must be orderly and short, and he often reminded them not to shout or preach so long:

[1] *Letters*, vol. vi, pp. 156–8.   [2] *Ibid.*, vol. iii, p. 76.

Avoid all those strong, rhetorical exclamations, 'Oh horrid! Oh dreadful!' and the like, unless when you are strongly exhorting sinners to renounce the devil and all his works.[1]

To John King, who had considerable success preaching in America and of whom it was said that when preaching 'he made the dust fly from the old velvet cushions', Wesley wrote:

Scream no more, at the peril of your soul. God now warns you by me whom He has set over you. Speak as earnestly as you can, but do not scream. Speak with all your heart, but with a moderate voice.[2]

Keep sacredly to the Methodist rules. Conclude the service in an hour.[3]

Sometimes his commands were more exceptional, as when he wrote to George Holder:

I exceedingly disapprove of your publishing anything in the Manx language. On the contrary, we should do everything in our power to abolish it from the earth, and persuade every member of our Society to learn and talk English.[4]

How pointed and personal his remarks could be is shown in a letter to an Irish preacher giving a list of 'little things to remember':

(2) Be cleanly. In this let the Methodists take pattern by the Quakers. Avoid all nastiness, dirt, slovenliness, both in your person, clothes, house, and all about you. Do not stink above ground.

(3) Whatever clothes you have, let them be whole; no rents no tatters, no rags. . . . Mend your clothes, or I shall never expect you to mend your lives. Let none ever see a ragged Methodist. . . .

(7) Use no snuff unless prescribed by a physician. I suppose no other nation in Europe is in such vile bondage to this silly, nasty, dirty custom as the Irish are. . . .

(8) Touch no dram. It is liquid fire. . . . To this and snuff and smoky cabins I impute the blindness which is so exceedingly common throughout the nation.[5]

To Miss Bishop he expressed his dislike of 'enthusiastic' preaching and to excesses of emotion and rhetoric:

[1] *Letters*, vol. iv, p. 158. [2] *Ibid.*, vol. vi, p. 167.
[3] *Ibid.*, vol. vii, p. 313. [4] *Ibid.*, vol. viii, p. 189.
[5] *Ibid.*, vol. v, pp. 133-4.

I find more profit in sermons on either good temper or good works than in what are vulgarly called gospel sermons. The term is now become a mere *cant* word. I wish none of our Society would use it. It has no determinate meaning. Let but a pert, self-sufficient animal, that has neither sense nor grace, bawl out something about Christ and His Blood or justification by faith, and his hearers cry out, 'What a fine gospel sermon!' Surely the Methodists have not so learnt Christ. We know no gospel without salvation from sin.[1]

Possibly the best known of all his letters is that written to the Commissioners of Excise, who wrote for a statement of the plate in his possession as demanded by the Bill of 1776:

LONDON.
September, 1776.

SIR,—I have *two* silver tea-spoons at London, and *two* at Bristol. This is all the plate which I have at present; and I shall not buy any more while so many round me want bread.

I am, sir,
Your most humble servant.[2]

The shortest letters of the collection are these:

To Simon Day:
DEAR SIMON,—You shall be in Oxfordshire. Adieu.

To John White:
John White, whoever is wrong, you are not right.[3]

There is something moving in the brevity of some of the more serious letters. He decided in 1773 to send preachers to America, and wrote to George Shadford:

DEAR GEORGE,—The time is arrived for you to embark for America. You must go down to Bristol, where you will meet with Thomas Rankin, Captain Webb and his wife.

I let you loose, George, on the great continent of America. Publish your message in the open face of the sun, and do all the good you can.

I am, dear George,
Yours affectionately.[4]

With this might be compared the letter to William Black, who was working in Canada in 1784:

[1] *Letters*, vol. vi, p. 326.   [2] *Ibid.*, vol. vi, p. 230.
[3] *Ibid.*, vol. vii, pp. 219, 227.   [4] *Ibid.*, vol. vi, p. 23.

I do not expect we shall meet in this world. But you have a large field of action where you are without wandering into Europe. Your present parish is wide enough—namely, Nova Scotia and Newfoundland. I do not advise you to go any further.[1]

He never wrote with more telling intensity than he did in the letters of the last two years, and it is the picture of the old man that has won the hearts of all who have written about him. In his own time he was once more received everywhere with goodwill and acclamation, and all over the country pulpits were offered him again.

Lecky, who was not sympathetic to Methodism, was attracted by the charm of the old man. He wrote:

His style . . . is characterized above all things by its extreme directness, by the manifest and complete subordination of all other considerations to the one great end of impressing his doctrines on his hearers. . . . His manners and language were always those of a gentleman—calm, deliberate and self-possessed. He was always dressed with scrupulous neatness. His countenance, to the very close of his life, was singularly beautiful and expressive.[2]

Wesley's last letter to America, where Methodism spread rapidly after the War of Independence, was this:

February 1, 1791.

To Ezekiel Cooper of Philadelphia:

MY DEAR BROTHER,—Those that desire to write or say anything to me have no time to lose; for time has shaken me by the hand and death is not far behind. But I have reason to be thankful for the time that is past: I felt few of the infirmities of old age for fourscore and six years. It was not till a year and a half ago that my strength and my sight failed. And still I am enabled to scrawl a little, and to creep, though I cannot run. . . .

See that you never give place to one thought of separating from your brethren in Europe. Lose no opportunity of declaring to all men that the Methodists are one people in all the world; and that it is their full determination so to continue,

'Though mountains rise, and oceans roll,
    To sever us in vain.'

To the care of our common Lord I commit you; and am,

Your affectionate friend and brother.[3]

[1] *Letters*, vol. vii, p. 244.
[2] *England in the Eighteenth Century*, Lecky, vol. iii, p. 121.
[3] *Letters*, vol. viii, pp. 259-60.

It was fitting that the last important letter he wrote should have been to the young William Wilberforce who was just beginning his work. (Wesley signed two or three notes after this.)

February 24, 1791.

To William Wilberforce.

DEAR SIR,—Unless the Divine Power has raised you up to be as *Athanasius contra mundum*, I see not how you can go through your glorious enterprise in opposing that execrable villainy, which is the scandal of religion, of England, and of human nature. Unless God has raised you up for this very thing, you will be worn out by the opposition of men and devils. But if God be for you, who can be against you? Are all of them together stronger than God? O be not weary of well doing! Go on, in the name of God, and in the power of His might, till even American slavery (the vilest that ever saw the sun) shall vanish away before it.[1]

For other purposes in this book, other letters will be quoted, but enough examples have been given for the moment to illustrate their general style and tone. It would be foolish to claim that they have great literary values or that they are ever conscious works of art. They have never the expansive survey of current life and society gossip that make those of Horace Walpole of such interest, nor have they a single aim, like those of Lord Chesterfield to his son. Probably the best letters are written by people with plenty of leisure, who can set down their news and reflections in a personal manner, and allow the reader to see the writer's character behind the letter. This has given the world the 'divine chit-chat' of Charles Lamb and of William Cowper, while the importance of the views and development of poets like Keats and Gray have an interest outside the form of the letters. With none of these can the letters of John Wesley be directly compared.

The keynote of all his letters is purpose. He sat down to write to some one to give him instructions, advice, or help, and then wrote as clearly and briefly as was possible. This is true of his letters in general, though it would be foolish to assert that he could not elaborate when he thought necessary, or that he did not deal at sufficient length with any

[1] *Letters*, vol. viii, p. 265.

matter he had to discuss. His letters are never mere notes from a man in a hurry. His years of practice in presiding at the Disputations and summing up the arguments at Oxford gave him the ability to see clearly and to describe accurately what he saw. His views may be wrong, but he can explain them lucidly. To one of his preachers, Samuel Furly, he wrote many times stating his tastes in both preaching and writing, at times in words that recall Wordsworth's preface to the *Lyrical Ballads*. He certainly carried out his own advice in such a letter as the following:

> I doubt you had a dunce for a tutor at Cambridge, and so *set out* wrong. Did he never tell you that, of all men living, a clergyman should '*talk* with the vulgar'? yea, and *write* imitating the language of the *common people* throughout, so far as consists with purity and *propriety* of speech?
> *Easiness* therefore, is the first, second, and third point; and *stiffness*, *apparent* exactness, *artificialness* of style the main defect to be avoided, next to solecism and impropriety. . . . If you *will* imitate, imitate Mr. Addison or Dr. Swift.[1]

As examples of the qualities he admired, his letters can be read with pleasure to-day, and it is obvious that his views must have had considerable influence both on the written as well as the spoken words of his preachers. I shall show later on that the special characteristic which an unbiased critic like Dr. Johnson noted about the Methodist preachers was the plainness and directness of their style.

Wesley's most expansive and personal letters were generally written to women, and to them he could more easily tell of his own doubts and religious feelings, just as during the first half of his life all his most difficult problems were discussed with his mother. The letters to and from her reveal again and again what a truly remarkable woman she was. His letters to his preachers show how far he was typical of the gentlemen of his own time, how insistent he was on order, restraint and decorum, how, amidst scenes of emotional excess, when some of his followers would have imitated the excesses of mystics and of those 'who spoke with tongues', his was the voice that restrained and controlled them. The

---

[1] *Letters*, vol. iv, p. 232.

letters show, too, that a great many of his followers were also men and women of good education and of great ability.

In the *Letters*, more perhaps than in the *Journal*, Wesley's ironic wit shows itself, although he generally manages to keep it rigidly under control. Like him, others among his preachers studied and prayed hard to be preserved from 'levity', but it persisted in breaking in at strange moments. Sir Leslie Stephen has well described them:

It would be difficult to find any letters more direct, pithy, and forcible in expression. Wesley goes straight to the mark without one superfluous flourish. He writes as a man confined within the narrowest limits of time and space, whose thoughts are so well in hand that he can say everything needful within those limits. The compression gives emphasis and never causes confusion.[1]

But it is Wesley's most simple and personal statements that remain in the memory and which often give rise to his most telling phrases. The gossip of Horace Walpole and the excellent advice of Lord Chesterfield are appreciated by all who study the eighteenth century, but it seems a pity that many of Wesley's letters with their evidence of his undaunted courage and continual good temper should be little known.

With a knowledge of the life of the writer and of the background against which he wrote, letters such as that which follows seem of a unique type in English literature:

In the present journey I leap as broke from chains. I am content with whatever entertainment I meet with, and my companions are always in a good humour 'because they are with me'. This must be the spirit of all who take journeys with me. If a dinner ill-dressed, or hard bed, a poor room, a shower of rain, or a dusty road will put them out of humour, it lays a burthen upon me greater than all the rest put together.

By the grace of God I never fret, I repine at nothing, I am discontented with nothing. And to hear persons at my ear fretting and murmuring at everything is like tearing the flesh off my bones. I see God sitting upon His throne and ruling all things well.[2]

[1] *English Thought in the Eighteenth Century*, Leslie Stephen, vol. ii, p. 410.
[2] *Letters*, vol. iii, pp. 138-9.

THE CONTROVERSIAL AND POLITICAL WORKS OF JOHN WESLEY

Controversial writings. Advice to Methodists. Rules. Tracts and Political Writings. The Sermons.

(Most of the references are taken from *The Works of the Rev. John Wesley*, *A.M.* Edited Thomas Jackson. Fourteen vols. Third Edition, 1829–31.)

Chapter III

THE CONTROVERSIAL AND POLITICAL WORKS
OF JOHN WESLEY

> Besides the rest, which we assert as facts,
> He wrote in all above Two Hundred Tracts!
> And yet, in ev'ry year, a Thousand Missives sent
> Through this, and various Isles, and ev'ry Continent!

So wrote Thomas Olivers in his *Descriptive and Plaintive Elegy on the late Reverend John Wesley*, published just after his death.[1] The word 'tracts' is, however, hardly adequate for Wesley's enormous publications. Richard Green, in his *Wesley Bibliography*, has 425 publications for John and Charles, and certainly the great majority belong to John. Some of these publications ran into as many as twenty editions.

Wesley is said to have made between £30,000 and £40,000 profit on the sale of these books; but this was all spent on his work or given away in the social work done by his centres. His printing and publishing house in City Road continues to-day and is now the oldest printing house to have run continuously in London.

Wesley's educational books and his editions of novels and anthologies of verse will be considered in the next chapter, but his own prose works may be roughly divided into four sections.

Firstly, there are numerous books and pamphlets explaining what Methodism was, elucidating difficulties to the public and appealing for a fair and critical examination of the whole movement. A good example of this kind is *An Earnest Appeal to Men of Reason and Religion*. Secondly, there are the various sets of rules and regulations published for his own followers. These grew and were expanded as

[1] See chap. viii.

time went on, and are shown best in *The Large Minutes*. Thirdly, there are what may truly be called 'tracts', short publications printed in thousands to be sold cheaply or given away. These include pamphlets addressed to the inhabitants of England and Ireland in times of special emergency, such as the earthquake scare of 1755, and at the time of fear of a French invasion, and tracts on political matters, such as the shortage of food, the slave trade, and the American rebellion. Under this section fall such papers as *A Word to a Smuggler*, *A Word to a Condemned Malefactor*, *A Word to a Drunkard*, and *A Word to a Swearer*. Lastly, there are the sermons.

Of this vast mass of writings, Leslie Stephen has said that throughout—

Wesley remains on the plane of terse, vigorous sense. But it is also true that his eloquence never soars above the ground; and if there is no bombast, there is little more rhetoric than may be found in a vigorous leading article, and if he wins our respect he does not excite our admiration, or add to the stores of English rhetorical prose. . . . His English is allied to that of Swift or Arbuthnot; but unluckily, his thoughts run so frequently in the grooves of obsolete theological speculation that he has succeeded in producing no single book satisfactory in a literary sense.[1]

Possibly the last sentence is just, and no single book is satisfactory as pure literature: but much of the rest of this extract needs considerable modification before passing as a final judgement of Wesley's works. There are many parts of most of these that are still of great interest, not only because of their content, but also from their manner of expression. The actual amount of 'theological speculation' is small.

It is intended here to take a few examples from each of the suggested classes and give quotations to show their interest and merit.

In the early days of the Methodist movement, when violent attacks were made on it by pamphlets and journals, Wesley replied in a forty-page pamphlet, *An Earnest Appeal to Men of Reason and Religion*. In this he tried to examine the state of the country and to give an account of what he was

[1] *English Thought in the Eighteenth Century*, Leslie Stephen, vol. ii, p. 411.

preaching, in order to show that in doctrine he nowhere
differed from the Church of England to which he belonged.
He pointed out that what he insisted upon from those who
chose to follow him was a strict ethical standard and not
certain opinions. He also dealt briefly with some of the
charges levelled against him, such as those accusing him of
being a Papist in disguise, being a Quaker, trying to destroy
the Church of England, seeking fame, and being a fortune-
hunter. The quotations below give some impression of his
stress on reason to which he tried to bring all his arguments.
The sketch of the daily life of the aristocracy and its comparison with that of the Indians in Georgia is a good example
of his powers of writing vivid, direct, colloquial English:

Are you now happy? I have seen a large company of reasonable
creatures, called Indians, sitting in a row on the side of a river,
looking sometimes at one another, sometimes at the sky, and sometimes at the bubbles on the water. And so they sat (unless in time
of war) for a great part of the year, from morning to night. These
were doubtless much at ease. But can you think they were happy?
And how much happier are you than they? You eat, and drink,
and sleep, and dress, and dance, and sit down to play. You are
carried abroad. You are at the masquerade, the theatre, the opera-
house, the park, the levee, the drawing-room. What do you do there?
Why, sometimes you talk; sometimes you look at one another. And
what are you to do to-morrow, the next day, the next week, the next
year? You are to eat, and drink, and dance, and dress, and play
again. And you are to be carried abroad again, that you may look
at one another. And is this all? Alas! how little more happiness
have you in this, than the Indians in looking at the sky or water! . . .
Are you, can you, or any reasonable man be satisfied with this?
It is plain you do not love God. If you did, you would be happy
in him.[1]

The following year Wesley replied to further charges made
against him, and in particular to that made by the Archbishop of York, who had sent an anonymous pamphlet to all
his clergy, entitled *Observations on the Conduct and Behaviour of
a Certain Sect usually Distinguished by the Name of Methodists.*
He had grown very rhetorical in his attack on their 'enthusiasm'. Wesley replied in *A Farther Appeal to Men of Reason and
Religion*, and in it said:

[1] *Works*, vol. viii, pp. 3–19.

[This pamphlet] has been generally supposed to be wrote by a person who is in every way my superior. Perhaps one reason why he did not inscribe his name was, that his greatness might not make me afraid; and that I might have liberty to stand as it were on even ground, while I answer for myself. . . .

Before I take my leave I cannot but recommend to you that advice of a wise and good man:

> 'Be calm in arguing; for fierceness makes
> Error a fault, and truth discourtesy.'

I am grieved at your extreme warmth: You are in a thorough ill humour from the very beginning of your book to the end. This cannot hurt me; but it may yourself. And it does not at all help your cause. If you denounce against me all the curses from Genesis to the Revelation, they will not amount to one argument. I am willing (as far as I know myself) to be reproved either by you or by any other. But whatever you do, let it be done in love, in patience, in meekness of wisdom. . . .[1]

In the second part of this *Farther Appeal*, he examined the argument that England was already a Christian country and needed nothing further. Wesley argued that if this were true, he could examine the great institutions of the land and be satisfied, so he turned to the hospitals, to Ludgate, and to Newgate, of which he says: 'I know not if, to one of a thinking sensible turn of mind, there could be anything like it on this side of hell.' Next he examined the different religious bodies of the country and gave a sketch of the conditions of each, stressing their characteristic merits and defects. Some of these are reminiscent of the character sketches of William Law. For an example, here is that of a Quaker who boasted of his plainness of speech, but Wesley objected that real plainness does not lie in certain customs and mannerisms but in undisguised sincerity. Again his powers of irony are displayed, as well as his ability to turn a Scriptural phrase neatly:

For instance: This woman is too strict a Quaker to lay out a shilling in a necklace. Very well; but she is not too strict to lay out fourscore guineas in a repeating watch. Another would not for the world wear any lace; no, not an edging round her cap: But she will wear point, and sees no harm in it at all, though it should be of twelve times the price. . . . And what multitudes of you are very jealous, as

[1] *Works*, vol. viii, pp. 59, 76.

to the colour and form of your apparel, (the least important of all the circumstances that relate to it,) while in the most important, the expense, they are without any concern at all? They will not put on a scarlet or crimson stuff, but the richest velvet, so it be black or grave. They will not touch a coloured riband; but will cover themselves with stiff silk from head to foot. They cannot bear purple; but make no scruple at all of being clothed in fine linen; yea, to such a degree, that the linen of the Quakers is grown almost into a proverb.[1]

He exhorted all sects to obey strictly the best rules of their creed, the Roman Catholics being told to read Thomas à Kempis and the Marquis de Renty. Finally, he turned to those who had no religion:

You seek happiness. But you find it not. You come no nearer it with all your labours. You are not happier than you was a year ago. . . . Indeed, what is there on earth which can long satisfy a man of understanding? His soul is too large for the world he lives in. He wants more room.[2]

Wesley was certainly the master of a fine phrase when he required it. Enough has probably been quoted to show that much of Wesley's prose had little to do with 'obsolete theological speculation'. In fact, his aims were nearly always practical and ethical rather than speculative and he generally drove in his points with homely similes and illustrations. Nor can a mastery of rhetorical prose be wholly denied him. For an example of this, we might take an extract from the third part of *A Farther Appeal*, written during the scare of the rebellion of 1745. The two foes, Jacobitism and ungodliness, were curiously related in Wesley's mind:

Honest neighbour, do not be angry. Lay down your hammer, and let us talk a little on this head. They have no conception of piety without loyalty. . . .
The mariner may have many concerns to mind, and many businesses to engage his thoughts; but not when the ship is sinking. In such a circumstance (it is your own) you have but one thing to think of,—save the ship and your own life together!
And the higher post you are in, the more deeply intent should you be on this one point. Is this a time for diversions; for eating and drinking, and rising up to play? Keep the ship above water. Let all else go, and mind this one thing!

[1] *Works*, vol. viii, p. 186.   [2] *Ibid*., vol. viii, p. 193.

Perhaps you will say, 'So I do: I do mind this one thing,—how to save the sinking nation. And therefore now I must think of arms and provisions. I have no time now to think of religion'. This is exactly as if the mariner should say, 'Now I must think of my guns and stores. I have no time now to think of the hold'. Why, man, you must think of this or perish. It is there the leak is sprung. Stop that, or you and all your stores will go together to the bottom of the sea.[1]

Possibly this is passionate, colloquial English of great persuasive power rather than rhetoric. If Leslie Stephen had to be refuted in saying that no single work of Wesley's was satisfactory in a literary sense, the best book to offer in defence would be the three parts of *A Farther Appeal*. It has the best dispassionate analysis of English life of the time, with accounts of the different classes and sects and the growing spirit of dissatisfaction, of which I am aware. Nor is there that exaggeration of social evils which is prominent often in the sermons of different ages. It is not a view of English life black and cruel like that shown in the pictures of Hogarth, though incidentally there are glimpses of this; but it is a rational and seemingly accurate picture drawn by one who saw the root of the evil to be godlessness. Wesley is careful never to seem 'enthusiastic', and to base all his arguments on common sense and reason rather than on religious tenets. Examples will be given later on of the kind of abuse, rhetorical denunciation, and furious invective with which he was attacked, and the continued ridiculous charges that he had to meet. Wesley was like Defoe in many ways; for, as his opponents grew more violent and abusive, he grew calmer and more reasonable. He never lost his temper or good manners in his controversies, and it is nearly always the eighteenth-century apostles of good taste rather than the Methodist that seem to be foaming 'enthusiasts'.

Like Defoe again, as he begs his opponents to be reasonable, or to confute him by arguments and not by abuse, he turns for homely illustrations from everyday events to demonstrate his points. He seems to say that his argument is not vague or mystical, needing experts or learned men to

[1] *Works*, vol. viii, pp. 235, 240.

understand it, but simple common sense to be comprehended by the meanest intelligence, and easily illustrated by incidents which all know well: a beggar in the street, a man shouting at a meeting, a gentleman in his chair, or a storm at sea. To the furious assertions that he drives people mad, that he takes away the little money that the poor do possess, that his preachers are mere ranters, he calmly asks for details, for places and dates. Show me, he says, where this has happened, and I will put it right. Hostile charges were always drawn up 'on the notable foundation of hearsay', and continued abuse only threw into relief the seeming reasonableness of his argument.

Thus much of the controversial writing of John Wesley still keeps its interest, and, once read, the concrete imagery and the sharp incisive sentences are not soon forgotten. Behind the scrupulous politeness there is often a depth of irony and intensity of feeling that still transforms what at first seems to be worn-out theological ideas into matter of living interest.

. . . . .

The second class of the Wesley writings is that devoted to the rules or the advice given to various classes of his followers. These were issued from time to time and were expanded as conditions changed between 1744 and 1791. The best known edition is called *The Large Minutes*, and the quotations used here are all taken from the edition of 1791. Surprisingly enough, these form most interesting reading, and give vivid glimpses of the life of the time and the thoroughness of Wesley's discipline over those who chose to follow him *The Large Minutes* are in the form of questions and answers, and in these he states all kinds of objections to his rules before crushing them with decision and weight. Probably the best known section is that which answers Question 26:

Q. What are the rules of a Helper?
A. Be diligent. Never be unemployed a moment. Never be triflingly employed. Never while away time; neither spend any more time at any place than is strictly necessary.

2. Be serious. Let your motto be, 'Holiness to the Lord'. Avoid all lightness, jesting, and foolish talking.

3. Converse sparingly and cautiously with women; particularly, with young women.

4. Take no step toward marriage, without first consulting with your brethren.

5. Believe evil of no one; unless you see it done, take heed how you credit it. Put the best construction on everything. You know the Judge is always supposed to be on the prisoner's side.

6. Speak evil of no one; else your word especially would eat as doth a canker. Keep your thoughts within your own breast, till you come to the person concerned.

7. Tell every one what you think wrong in him, and that plainly, as soon as may be; else it will fester in your heart. Make all haste to cast the fire out of your bosom.

8. Do not affect the gentleman. You have no more to do with this character than with that of a dancing master. A Preacher of the gospel is the servant of all.

9. Be ashamed of nothing but sin: Not of fetching wood (if time permit) or drawing water; not of cleaning your own shoes, or your neighbour's.

10. Be punctual. Do everything exactly at the time. And, in general, do not mend our Rules, but keep them; not for wrath, but for conscience' sake.

11. You have nothing to do but to save souls. Therefore spend and be spent in this work. And go always, not only to those that want you, but to those that want you most. . . .

Observe: . . . A Methodist Preacher is to mind every point, great and small, in the Methodist discipline! Therefore you will need all the sense you have, and to have all your wits about you![1]

The rigorous rules for the study and reading of his preachers, with the list of books to be treated, are examined elsewhere, and it is not intended to recount here any of his more theological suggestions. He added, however, some 'smaller advices relative to preaching' which show his insistence on order and restraint and his abhorrence of excesses and peculiarity of behaviour. Some only are quoted here:

2. Begin and end precisely at the time appointed.

3. Let your whole deportment before the congregation be serious, weighty and solemn. . . .

6. Take care not to ramble; but keep to your text and make out what you take in hand.

7. Be sparing in allegorizing and spiritualizing.

8. Take care of anything awkward or affected, either in your gesture, phrase or pronunciation.

[1] *Works*, vol. viii, pp. 309–10.

9. Sing no hymns of your own composing.
10. Print nothing without my approbation. . . .
13. In repeating the Lord's Prayer, remember to say, '*Hallowed* not *hollowed*; trespass against *us*': 'Amen'. . . .
18. Avoid quaint words; however in fashion, as *object*, *originate*, *very*, *high*, &c.
19. Avoid the fashionable impropriety of leaving out the *u* in many words, as *honor*, *vigor*, &c. This is mere childish affectation.
20. Beware of clownishness, either in speech or dress. Wear no slouched hat.
21. Be merciful to your beast. Not only ride moderately, but see with your own eyes that your horse be rubbed, fed, and bedded.[1]

Wesley's own views on singing and the use of music in services were just as decided, and he gave detailed instructions for the meetings of his society. The hymns were to be kept to strict time, and sensible tunes were always to be used; but they were to avoid certain fashions in anthems. An evil called 'formality' crept in with certain anthems:

Is not this formality creeping in already, by those complex tunes, which it is scarcely possible to sing with devotion? Such is 'Praise the Lord, ye blessed ones'. Such the long quavering hallelujah annexed to the morning-song tune, which I defy any man living to sing devoutly. The repeating the same words so often, (but especially while another repeats different words, the horrid abuse which runs through the modern church music,) as it shocks all common sense, so it necessarily brings in dead formality, and has no more religion in it than a Lancashire hornpipe. Besides, it is a flat contradiction of our Lord's command, 'Use not vain repetitions'. For what is a vain repetition, if this is not? What end of devotion does it serve? Sing no anthems.[2]

The Methodists seemed to take little notice of his commands about anthems, and some chapels became famous for their choirs.

Finally, the list of questions for the self-examination of his preachers ought to be glanced at, to show the Spartan life that Wesley demanded, as well as his deep knowledge of human nature. These questions are searching and personal, and he who could answer firmly and virtuously each one must indeed have been worthy of his calling. It makes quite

[1] *Works*, vol. viii, p. 317.   [2] *Ibid.*, vol. viii, p. 318.

humorous reading when we see the way he nails them down to exact weaknesses and counters each excuse they might offer to make. Once the weakness is acknowledged, the reformation must be soon—in fact, it must begin at that very moment. For example, the questions for the end of the day may be taken, when the preacher might feel like resting and seeking comfort over a good meal:

> Do you eat no flesh suppers? . . . no late suppers? . . . Do you eat no more at each meal than is necessary? . . . Are you not heavy or drowsy after dinner? . . . Do you drink water? . . . Why not? . . . Did you ever? . . . Why did you leave it off? . . . If not for health, when will you begin again? . . . to-day? . . .[1]

. . . . .

In the third class of Wesley's writings which have been labelled for convenience his 'tracts', the quantity and variety is almost bewildering. Many of them, however, are based on the political issues of the time, of which one of the strongest was the cry for liberty. In the middle of the century, criticism of the rule of George II and George III and their Ministers grew in strength, and John Wilkes and Charles Churchill formed the point of the attack. Ideas from Voltaire and Rousseau were entering English life and being echoed by pamphlets, while papers like *The North Briton* proved that popular opinion could do much to overthrow a government. Then Junius came and public interest was further increased. The watchword of the whole movement was 'Liberty'.

How nearly allied in essentials Methodism was to this movement Wesley never realized,[2] for politically he was strongly opposed to this new liberal opinion. He believed that he lived in a country which had every possible liberty, and which was governed by the best possible King. Thus, he regarded Junius and Wilkes as enemies to their country and thought that they were probably seduced by French gold. Many pamphlets, such as *Thoughts on the State of Public Affairs*, *Thoughts Upon Liberty*, *Thoughts concerning the Origin*

[1] *Works*, vol. viii, p. 324.
[2] The social implications of Methodism are briefly considered in the last chapter.

of Power, and *A Serious Address to the People of England,* all contain these views, but a short quotation from *Thoughts upon Liberty* will serve best to illustrate it. After two lines from Prior—

> I scorn to have my free-born toe
> Dragoon'd into a wooden shoe—

he proceeded to show that men were everywhere crying for Liberty:

> Who can deny that the whole kingdom is panting for liberty? . . . Liberty! Liberty! sounds through every county, every city, every town, and every hamlet. Is it not for the sake of this, that the name of our great patriot . . . is more celebrated than that of any private man has been in England for these thousand years; that his very picture is so joyfully received in every part of England and Ireland; that we stamp his (I had almost said, adored) name on our hand-kerchiefs, on the cheerful bowl, yea, and on our vessels of various kinds, as well as upon our hearts? . . .
>
> In the name of wonder, what religious liberty can you desire, or even conceive, which you have not already? Where is there a nation in Europe, in the habitable world, which enjoys such liberty of conscience as the English? . . .
>
> What is it you are making all this pother about? Why are you thus wringing your hands and screaming, to the terror of your quiet neighbours, 'Destruction! Slavery! Bondage! Help, countrymen! Our liberty is destroyed! We are ruined, chained, fettered, undone!'
>
> *Fettered!* How? Where are the fetters, but in your own imagination? There are none, either on your hands or mine: neither you nor I can show to any man in his senses, that we have one chain upon us, even so big as a knitting needle.[1]

It was in the middle of the agitation for Liberty that the American question arose. English liberal opinion favoured the cause of the Colonists or generally sympathized with them, and for a time at the onset Wesley agreed with them. His letter to the Secretary of State for the Colonies and to Lord North has already been quoted,[2] and it may be recalled that there he pleaded for concessions for the Colonists and pointed out the impossibility of coercing them, even if it was desirable. Then he read Dr. Johnson's *Taxation No Tyranny,* which converted him to the Government

[1] *Works,* vol. xi, pp. 34–42. [2] Chap. ii.

view. To help the Government and if possible to gain a circulation in America, Wesley extracted arguments and passages from Johnson's tract and republished it under the title, *A Calm Address to Our American Colonies*. He added an application to 'those whom it most concerns'. This pamphlet, consisting of four pages, was sold for 1*d.* in England, and a vast number was sent to America. The copies sent there, however, were never distributed, possibly being destroyed by the authorities there or by Methodist friends who feared that the views expressed would be too unpopular. Wesley's attitude was known in America and for a long time his preachers were in danger of their lives.. His account of the fate of this tract is as follows, and suggests that few copies ever left England:

About a year and a half ago, being exceedingly pained at what I saw or heard continually, I wrote a little tract entitled *A Calm Address to Our American Colonies*; but the ports being then shut up by the Americans, I could not send it abroad as I designed. However, it was not lost; within a few months, fifty, or perhaps an hundred thousand copies, in newspapers and otherwise, were dispersed throughout Great Britain and Ireland.[1]

The English Nonconformists were mostly supporters of the American cause, and these joined with others who sympathized with the Colonists to attack Wesley. Sheaves of pamphlets were published, many containing bitter personal attacks as well as accusations of betraying his cause by changing sides.[2] Wesley issued another edition of his pamphlet with slight emendations, and his friend, Fletcher of Madeley, published answers and defences of both Wesley and the Government. The controversy is of interest as showing the complete separation between the Methodists, a kind of branch of the Church of England, and the Nonconformists of the time. The *Calm Address to Our American Colonies* began:

I was of a different judgement on this head till I read a tract entitled *Taxation no Tyranny*. But as soon as I received more light myself, I judged it my duty to impart it to others. I therefore

[1] *Works*, vol. xi, p. 129.   [2] See chap. x.

extracted the chief arguments from the treatise, and added an application to those whom it most concerns. I was well aware of the treatment this would bring upon myself; but let it be, so I may in any degree serve my King and country.[1]

Wesley then satirized the 'florid rhetoric' and overstatements that had characterized the replies to Dr. Johnson, and said:

The writer asserts twenty times, 'He that is taxed without his own consent, that is, without being represented, is a slave'. I answer, No; I have no representative in Parliament; but I am taxed; yet I am no slave. Yea, nine in ten throughout England have no representative, no vote; yet they are no slaves; they enjoy both civil and religious liberty to the utmost extent.[2]

He had seen real slavery in Georgia and had little sympathy with those who used the word loosely. 'Is not all this outcry about liberty and slavery mere rant and playing upon words?' he asked, before concluding his introduction: 'I now speak according to the light I have. But if anyone will give me more light, I will be thankful.'[3]

All the tracts show Wesley's exhortations for loyalty and obedience to the Crown and his insistence on exact fulfilment of the law of the land. This cut Methodism off from the growing radical and revolutionary movement as well as from the Dissenters who generally had liberal opinions or desired more liberty.

The shorter tracts are ethical rather than religious in tone, if such an antithesis be possible. Thus a pamphlet, *A Word to a Smuggler*, was circulated in Cornwall and around the South Coast, where even strict and religious people were inclined not to ask questions when buying their wines and lace. About this matter Wesley was trenchant, using his method of short, pointed questions and answers. After dealing with the romantic picture of smugglers, and insisting that they were neither picturesque nor poor tradesmen trying to provide for their families, he concluded:

Open smugglers are worse than common highwaymen, and private smugglers are worse than common pickpockets. . . .

[1] *Works*, vol. xi, p. 80.   [2] *Ibid.*, vol. xi, p. 81.
[3] Dr. Johnson's attitude towards Wesley's tract is discussed in chap. x.

'But I only buy a little brandy or tea now and then, just for my own use.' That is, I only steal a little. God says, 'Steal not at all'.

'Why, I would not meddle with it, but I am forced by my parent, husband, or master.' If you are forced by your father or mother to rob, you will be hanged nevertheless. This may lessen, but does not take away the fault; for you ought to suffer rather than sin.

'But I do not know that it was run.' No! Did not he that sold it tell you it was? If he sold it under the common price, he did. The naming the price was telling you, 'This is run.'[1]

The slave trade drew forth his most impassioned prose, and when the Society for the Abolition of Slavery was formed, Wesley sent them letters of practical advice and issued tracts in their support. In *Thoughts upon Slavery*, in 1774, he discussed the whole question and reviewed the history of slavery from the earliest times. He quoted from the official French reports to prove that in Africa itself the black men lived happily and healthily, were well behaved, peaceable, and religious. Slave-traders argued that they removed the negroes from Africa for their own good. Next he gave an account of the methods employed to secure the slaves in Africa, and described the horrors of the sea voyage to America. Generally he maintained a cool, logical account of the happenings, but towards the close his feelings overcame him and passion broke through his reserve:

Mr. Anderson in his *History of Trade and Commerce*, observes: 'England supplies her American colonies with Negro slaves, amounting in number to about an hundred thousand a year;' that is, so many are taken aboard our ships; but at least ten thousand of them die in the voyage; about a fourth part more die at the different islands, in what is called seasoning. So that at an average, in the passage and seasoning together, thirty thousand die; that is, properly, are murdered. O Earth, O Sea, cover not thou their blood![2]

From his own experience in Georgia, Wesley was able to back up the accounts given by Sir Hans Sloane of the cruelty inflicted on slaves working in America, and to quote passages about inhuman punishments from the American newspapers. Next he examined the theory that slaves had to

---

[1] *Works*, vol. xi, pp. 174–8.   [2] *Ibid.*, vol. xi, p. 67.

be imported into America because white men could not do work there on account of the climate. This was untrue, said Wesley, because he himself had worked in the heat of Georgia. He claimed that white men were healthiest in hot lands when they did work each day, and that sweating from manual labour prevented disease. This theory seems to anticipate the results of modern research. Finally, he quoted the words of a Member of Parliament, 'Damn justice: it's a necessity'.

> I answer, you stumble at the threshold; I deny that villainy is ever necessary. It is impossible that it should ever be necessary for any reasonable creature to violate all the laws of justice, mercy, and truth. No circumstances can make it necessary for a man to burst in sunder all the ties of humanity. It can never be necessary for a rational creature to sink himself below a brute.[1]

Enough has now been quoted, probably, to illustrate the general attitude of Wesley to the events and movements of his time, and to show the vigour and clarity of his prose. Far from appearing dull and musty, the topics about which Wesley wrote seem to take on new life and interest when read again to-day, and it becomes possible to understand the recent French critic who has said: 'The social influence of Methodist ideas in England cannot be overestimated.'[2]

In the *Collected Works* of John Wesley are three volumes containing in all 141 sermons.[3] To Methodists, forty-four of these are of greater importance than the rest, because when in 1763 Wesley had to draw up a model deed for his preaching houses, it was provided that persons appointed by the Conference should 'have and enjoy the premises' only on condition 'that the said persons preach no other doctrine than is contained in Mr. Wesley's Notes upon the New Testament and the four volumes of sermons'. These volumes had

[1] *Works*, vol. xi, p. 72. This pamphlet on slavery received a detailed and very favourable review in the *Monthly Review* for 1774. A letter said to be by a resident in America cast doubts on the charges of cruelty to slaves there. The writer had never seen or heard of anything like it. Wesley replied by giving dated Advertisements which had appeared in American papers, offering rewards and describing the penalties for runaway slaves.

[2] *A History of English Literature*, by L. Cazamian, p. 955.

[3] *The Works of the Rev. John Wesley*, vols. v, vi, vii.

appeared in 1746, 1748, 1750, and 1760.[1] The Preface to the volume of 1746 states his aims in his usual clear, colloquial manner:

> The following Sermons contain the substance of what I have been preaching for between eight and nine years last past. . . .
> I design plain truth for plain people: therefore, of set purpose, I abstain from all nice and philosophical speculations; from all perplexed and intricate reasonings. . . . I labour to avoid all words which are not easy to be understood, all which are not used in common life. . . .
> I have accordingly set down in the following sermons what I find in the Bible concerning the way to heaven.

Later in the Preface, he deals with those who may disagree with him, developing that characteristic vein of irony that frequently appears in his prefaces:

> Are you persuaded you see more clearly than me? It is not unlikely that you may. Then treat me as you would desire to be treated yourself upon a change of circumstances. Point me out a better way than I have yet known. . . .
> For God's sake if it be possible to avoid it, let us not provoke one another to wrath.[2]

The style of this Preface, which is surely a fine piece of prose, is typical of the sermons themselves. They are always clear, reasonable, logical, and quiet. Writers who have pictured Wesley as an emotional, oratorical preacher who moved his crowds by rhetoric and terrified them by threats of hell fire, can find no justification for their views in the sermons. I have no doubt that their power lay in the apparent reasonableness and quiet sincerity of all he said. At times there seems no escape from his relentless logic as he drives home each point, using the simplest and most homely metaphors and similes to illustrate his statements. Just as Swift's satire almost

---

[1] In this book, unless otherwise stated, I have used the carefully edited and annotated edition of these forty-four sermons: *Wesley's Standard Sermons*, edited E. H. Sugden, two vols., 1921. It is interesting to note that there are no tests of doctrine for Methodist membership, but that there is a standard for preachers. These can believe what they like, but must not preach contrary views to those expressed in the *Sermons*. Rigidity is avoided because Wesley allowed for development in views and expressed willingness to alter opinions when he received greater light. See Introduction to *Standard Sermons*.

[2] *Standard Sermons*, 1921, vol. i, pp. 30–4.

appals by its quietness, so Wesley seems to grow calmer and more reasonable as he comes to his main arguments. It was probably this personal application of his tests, this keen spiritual diagnosis couched in colloquial language that could not be misunderstood, that affected his hearers so strongly in the eighteenth century.

Though some of the *Standard Sermons* were carefully planned to illustrate points of doctrine which Wesley considered needed particular stress, such as justification by faith, the means of grace, the catholic spirit, Christian perfection, a reading through of the list of titles of the sermons shows that he generally preached on very practical matters and frequently on simple morality and ethics. There are thirteen sermons on the application of the Sermon on the Mount, and many on such subjects as Self-Denial, the Use of Money, Evil-Speaking, a Caution against Bigotry, on Dress, on the Danger of Riches, on the Education of Children, on Obedience to Parents, on Visiting the Sick, on Worldly Folly, on the Reformation of Manners.

While avoiding theological matters, some quotations of the *Sermons* ought to be given, so finally I have chosen the sermon on the text, 'Redeeming the time' (Ephesians v. 16), to serve as an illustration. His use of short, pithy sentences, and his habit of stating the excuses of the weak before firmly suppressing them, is well shown. If not of his ordinary theology, the sermon is a good example of Wesley's use of English:

> I purpose, at present, to consider only one particular way of 'redeeming the time', namely, from sleep. This appears to have been exceeding little considered even by pious men. Many that have been eminently conscientious in other respects, have not been so in this. . . .
>
> That we may have a more just conception hereof, I will endeavour to show,
>
>   1. What it is to redeem the time from sleep.
>   2. The evil of not redeeming it. And,
>   3. The most effectual manner of doing it. . . .
>
> And I have long observed, that women, in general, want a little more sleep than men; perhaps, because they are, in common, of a weaker as well as a moister, habit of body. . . . Healthy men, in

general, need a little above six hours' sleep, healthy women, a little above seven, in four and twenty. I myself want six hours and a half, and I cannot well subsist with less.

After showing how to find the exact amount of sleep required, he proceeds to show that oversleeping hurts the health, softens the body, weakens the sight, and hurts the soul. Finally he comes to the cure:

I advise you, Thirdly, add to your faith, prudence: Use the most rational means to attain your purpose. Particularly begin at the right end, otherwise you will lose your labour. If you desire to rise early, sleep early; secure this point at all events. In spite of the most dear and agreeable companions, in spite of their most earnest solicitations, in spite of entreaties, railleries, or reproaches, rigorously keep your hour. Rise up precisely at your time, and retire without ceremony. Keep your hour, notwithstanding the most pressing business: Lay all things by till the morning. Be it ever so great a cross, ever so great self-denial, keep your hour, or all is over.

I advise you, Fourthly, be steady. Keep your hour of rising without intermission. Do not rise two mornings, and lie in bed the third; but what you do once, do always. 'But my head aches.' Do not regard that. It will soon be over. 'But I am uncommonly drowsy; my eyes are quite heavy.' Then you must not parley; otherwise it is a lost case; but start up at once. . . .

Perhaps you will say, 'The advice is good; but it comes too late! I have made a breach already. I did rise constantly for a season; nothing hindered me. But I gave way little by little, and I have now left it off for a considerable time'. Then, in the name of God, begin again! Begin to-morrow; or rather to-night, by going to bed early in spite of either company or business. . . .

But do not imagine that this single point, rising early, will suffice to make you a Christian. . . . It is but one step out of many; but it is one. And having taken this, go forward. Go on to universal self-denial, to temperance in all things, to a firm resolution of taking up daily every cross whereto you are called. Go on, in a full pursuit of all the mind that was in Christ, of inward and then outward holiness; so shall you be not almost but altogether a Christian; so shall you finish your course with joy: You shall wake up after his likeness, and be satisfied.[1]

[1] *Works*, vol. vii, pp. 67–75.

EDUCATIONAL AND LITERARY PUBLICATIONS OF JOHN WESLEY

Grammars and histories. The Dictionary. The anthology of verse. The novel. The *Magazine*. The Christian Library.

Fм

Chapter IV

EDUCATIONAL AND LITERARY PUBLICATIONS
OF JOHN WESLEY

To the question, 'What general method of employing our time would you advise us to?' Wesley replied to his preachers:

From six in the morning till twelve, (allowing an hour for breakfast,) to read in order with much prayer, first 'The Christian Library', and the other books which we have published in prose and verse, and then those which we recommended in our rules of Kingswood School. . . . Read the most useful books, and that regularly and constantly. Steadily spend all the morning in this employ, or, at least, five hours in four and twenty.[1]

To the reply of the weaker members, 'But I have no taste for reading', Wesley retorted, 'Contract a taste for it by use, or return to your trade'.

His preachers were expected to have their saddle-bags full of books, and all the chief preaching centres sold them. For the use of his preachers and members of the society, as well as for the use of the boys at Kingswood, Wesley re-issued many well-known works with explanatory notes. It will be impossible to do more here than glance at a few of them, because of their quantity.

There are five grammars: English, French, Latin, Greek, and Hebrew. These are quite short and cover only the more important points. *The Concise Ecclesiastical History* in four volumes, the *Concise History of England from the Earliest Times to the Death of George II, A Survey of the Wisdom of God in the Creation, or a Compendium of Natural Philosophy* in five volumes, are chiefly abstracts from the works of other writers. Wesley's method was to read what he considered to be the

---

[1] 'The Large Minutes,' *Works*, vol. viii, p. 313.

best books on the subject, and then to extract the more important passages and summarize their arguments. In the Preface to the *Ecclesiastical History* he explains what he has done:

> Many of the sentences are far too long, spun out with abundance of unnecessary words. . . . Sallust, not Cicero, is the standard for the style of a History. This I have studiously endeavoured to correct, by paring off the superfluity of words, and leaving only so many in every sentence, as sufficed to convey the meaning of it.

Again, in the *Natural Philosophy*, he says he has summarized the works of Dr. Goldsmith[1] and other writers, because he had long wanted to see an adequate book on the subject, which should be 'in the plainest dress: simply and nakedly expressed, in the most clear, easy and intelligible manner . . . free from the jargon of Mathematics which is mere heathen Greek to common readers'.

He found that commentaries on the Bible were all too dear for ordinary people to buy them, and that the cheap ones were of little value. Thus he took Matthew Henry's commentary[2] for his base, and added notes from 'Mr. Pool',[3] and from his own wider reading. Of Matthew Henry's work, Wesley writes:

> I not only omit much more than nineteen parts out of twenty of what he has written, but make many alterations and many additions wellnigh from the beginning to the end. . . . I likewise omit great part of every note the sum of which is retained; as it seems to be his aim to say as much, whereas it is mine to say as little, as possible. . . . It is no part of my design to save either learned or unlearned men from the trouble of thinking. . . . On the contrary, my intention is to make them think, and assist them in thinking.

In 1754 he issued *The New Testament with Explanatory Notes*. This was based on the best authority of the day, the

---

[1] *A Survey of the Wisdom of God in the Creation, or a Compendium of Natural Philosophy*, was first published in 1763 in two volumes. Wesley revised it and added a third volume in 1770. In 1777 he began to enlarge and revise this, when he saw Goldsmith's *An History of the Earth and Animated Nature*, which was published in June, 1774, two months after Goldsmith's death. Wesley admired this, 'and almost repented of having written anything on the subject'.

[2] *An Exposition of the Old and New Testament*, by Matthew Henry, late Minister of the Gospel: first published in 1706. It was still widely used in the nineteenth century.

[3] The book read was probably *Annotations upon the Holy Bible*, in English, by Matthew Poole, published posthumously in two volumes—1683-5. (This information was kindly given me by the Rev. F. Baker, B.A., B.D.)

Gnomon Novi Testamenti of Bengelius,[1] and included notes from the works of Dr. Guise, Dr. Heylin, and Dr. Doddridge. Wesley made a considerable number of changes in the text, chiefly from his own reading of the Greek. It is said that when he was at a loss for the correct words of any text in the Authorized Version, he could always remember the exact Greek rendering of it. It is no part of my intention to examine the changes introduced by Wesley, but it ought to be noted that recent investigators state that he anticipated the Revised Version in at least half of their changes, and 'nearly always in the more serious alterations. . . . And he anticipated them in the arrangement of the text into paragraphs'.[2]

Having given some account of the general principles upon which Wesley worked, I shall examine in more detail a few particular publications, and as a sample choose his *Dictionary*, his anthology of verse, and his edition of a novel.

In 1753 he brought out his *Dictionary*, and issued a second edition at Bristol in 1764. To this he added 'several hundreds of words chiefly from Mr. Johnson's *Dictionary*', which he had 'carefully looked over for that purpose'. Dr. Johnson's *Dictionary* had appeared in 1755. Wesley's *Dictionary* was a little book intended for the pocket and giving simple explanations of hard words. It consisted of only 144 pages, and the Preface showed Wesley in his more humorous and satirical mood. The title was:

The Complete English Dictionary, Explaining Most of those Hard Words, which are found in the best English Writers. By a Lover of Good English and Common Sense. N.B. The Author assures you, he thinks this is the best English Dictionary in the World.

In the Introduction, he says:

Incredible as it may appear, this dictionary is not published to get money, but to assist persons of common sense and no learning, to understand the best English authors, and that with as little expense of either time or money as the nature of the thing would allow.

[1] The Calvinistic *Gospel Magazine* referred to this in April, 1777: 'Bengelius's *Gnomon* (from whence Mr. Wesley has pilfered most of his wretched notes on the New Testament).' Wesley, however, had stated quite clearly from whence he had drawn his materials.

[2] *The Hymns of Methodism in their Literary Relations*, by Henry Bett, pp. 20–1.

(Greek, Latin, Legal, and technical terms have been omitted as well as such words as *and*, *of*, *but*, so that the book contains 'most of those hard words that are found in the best English writers'.)

I say *most*; for I purposely omit, not only all those that are not hard, and which are not found in the best writers; not only all law words, and most technical terms, but likewise all the meaning of which may be easily gathered from those of the same derivation. And this I have done to make this Dictionary both as short and as cheap as possible.

I should add no more, but that I have so often observed, the only way, according to modern taste, for any author to procure commendation to his book, is vehemently to commend it himself. For want of this deference to the public, several excellent tracts lately printed, but left to commend themselves by their own intrinsic worth, are utterly unknown or forgotten: Whereas if a writer of tolerable sense will but bestow a few violent encomiums on his own work, especially if they are skilfully ranged on the title-page; it will pass through six editions in a trice: The world being too complaisant to give a Gentleman the lie; and taking it for granted, he understands his own performance best.

In compliance, therefore, with the taste of the age, I add, that this little Dictionary is not only the shortest and cheapest, but likewise, by many degrees, the most correct, which is extant at this day. Many are the mistakes in all other English Dictionaries which I have yet seen: Whereas, I can truly say, I know of none in this: And I conceive the reader will believe me; for if I had, I should not have left it there. Use, then, this help, till you find a better.

The *Dictionary* certainly shows that Wesley observed his own rules and explained only the common, hard words. The letters X, Y, Z have only twelve words altogether. The letter A begins:

Abaft, behind, near the stern of a ship.
To abandon, to give up, resign, forsake.
To abase, to bring low.
To abash, to make ashamed.
An abbot, the chief of a convent.

Some interesting definitions are the following:

Deism, infidelity, denying the Bible.
Enthusiasm, religious madness, fancied inspiration.
Calvinists, they that hold absolute, unconditional Predestination.
Methodist, one that lives according to the method laid down in the Bible.

It may be recalled that the definition of a Methodist in Dr. Johnson's *Dictionary* was: 'One of the new kind of Puritans lately arisen, so called from their profession to live by rules and in constant method.'

Wesley's anthology of poetry was compiled at the request of the Countess of Huntingdon and was published in 1744. Its title was:

A Collection of Moral and Sacred Poems. From the most celebrated English Authors. By John Wesley, A.M., Fellow of Lincoln College, Oxford.

The first volume had 347 pages and the price unbound was 7s. 6d. The second and third volumes were published in the following year. In the Dedication to the Countess of Huntingdon, Wesley said that he had long had the design of attempting something of the kind, and that he had now revised all the English poems that he knew, and had selected what appeared most valuable in them, omitting only Spenser's works, 'because scarce intelligible to the generality of modern readers'. In this publication he followed his bad habit of not naming most of the authors of the poems. A recent critic has noted that Wesley chooses the best things from his authors and says the general selection 'does credit to his taste'.[1]

It is interesting, if a little trouble, to discover what authors he did choose and what space he gave to each. The first volume is the most varied and contains poems from the works of Milton, Sir John Davies, Herbert, Cowley, Roscommon, Yalden, Congreve, Dryden, Norris, Pomfret, Prior, Watts (many poems), Mrs. Rowe, Parnell, and Pope (fifty-eight pages). Volume II contains poems of Pope (twenty-three pages), Dryden, Young, Broome, Fitzgerald, Lewis, Dyer (fourteen pages), and Hughes. Volume III is nearly confined to the works of the Wesley family. Samuel Wesley, brother of John, has 134 pages and John and Charles occupy seventy-nine pages. The rest of the book has extracts from Herbert and Gambold.

Wesley, however, overstepped himself when publishing this anthology. He included ten pages of Young's *Night*

[1] Oliver Elton, *A Survey of English Literature, 1730–1780*. Vol. ii, p. 222.

Thoughts, which had only been published two years before. Dodsley owned the copyright of this and of Mrs. Rowe's[1] poems and began an action against Wesley for reprinting. Wesley received a Chancery bill,[2] 'a foul monster . . . a scroll of forty-two pages, in large folio, to tell a story which needed not to have taken forty lines'.[3] This seems to have increased his hatred of lawyers and legal forms; but he saw that he was in the wrong, and wrote to Dodsley to secure a settlement. They agreed on terms, and Wesley wrote to him:

LONDON.
February 8, 1745.

Having inadvertently printed in a collection of poems, 3 vols. 12mo, the *Night Thoughts* of Dr. Young, together with some pieces of Mrs. Rowe's the property of Mr. Robert Dodsley, and having made satisfaction for the same by payment of a £20 Bank Note, and a cheque for £30, payable in three months, I hereby promise not to print the same again in any form whatever.

JOHN WESLEY.[4]

Dodsley died in 1764 and Young in 1765. Thus any one could then print the poems, and in 1768 Wesley wrote in his *Journal*:

[1] Mrs. Elizabeth Rowe (1674–1737) had published poems in 1696, and had written an elegy on the death of her husband in 1715. After her death, Isaac Watts, in accordance with her wishes, published her *Devout Exercises of the Heart in Meditation and Soliloquy, Praise and Prayer*, 1737. This had many editions and was highly praised by Wesley in 1769 (*Journal*, vol. v, p. 326). Wesley probably selected her poems from *The Miscellaneous Works in Verse and Prose of Mrs. Rowe*, two vols., 1739.

[2] There is an account of the Wesley affair in *Robert Dodsley, Poet, Publisher and Playwright*, by Ralph Straus, 1910. This shows that by an agreement dated November 24, 1743, Young assigned the copyright of the first five parts of *Night Thoughts* to Dodsley for 160 guineas. On January 26, 1744, Dodsley bought the sixth part for 60 guineas. For some unknown reason, he did not publish the remaining three *Nights*, which were published by G. Hawkins, though the two men remained friends.

[3] *Journal*, vol. iii, p. 157. I have searched in the Public Records Office, but can find no trace of this bill. Possibly it was not kept when Wesley made his settlement. Wesley's dislike of lawyers and lawsuits is very marked in all his writings. He puts exclamation marks after phrases like, 'honest attorney'. He would have agreed heartily with John Pomfret in *The Choice*:

I'd be concerned in no litigious jaw; . . .
Lawsuits I'd shun, with as much studious care
As I would dens where hungry lions are;
And rather put up injuries, than be
A plague to him who'd be a plague to me.

[4] *Letters*, vol. ii, p. 27.

I took some pains in reading over Dr. Young's *Night Thoughts*, leaving out the indifferent lines, correcting many of the rest, and explaining the hard words, in order to make that noble work more useful to all and more intelligible to ordinary readers.[1]

Thus in 1770 he published at Bristol *An Extract from Dr. Young's 'Night Thoughts on Life, Death, and Immortality'*, and explained in his Preface that he had marked the 'sublimest passages of poetry'.

It might be noted here that he had already done this for *Paradise Lost* in 1763. With this he had omitted the passages which he considered too difficult to explain to ordinary readers, had appended notes on minor difficulties, and had marked with asterisks passages of peculiar excellence. In Books I and II, Milton has 1,910 lines, and of these Wesley includes 1,470 lines. Roughly one-third of the books were marked as peculiarly excellent, and Wesley recommended his readers to study these passages often, and suggested that many of his followers might learn them by heart. A second edition of *Paradise Lost* was published in 1791, while the *Night Thoughts* was re-issued several times after Wesley's death.

Wesley knew, however, that the taste of the majority of his followers was limited, and when writing to Walter Churchey, a friend of Cowper, he said:

The Methodists in general have very little taste for any poems but those of a religious or moral kind; and my brother has amply provided them with these.[2]

That they had a taste for poetry of this kind there can hardly be any doubt, when the large amount of poetry included in each issue of the *Arminian Magazine*, Wesley's anthology of verse, his issues of *Paradise Lost*, and Young's *Night Thoughts*, as well as his adaptations and re-issues of the works of George Herbert, is considered. His passion for re-issuing the books which he admired was only equalled by his belief in his ability to select their best parts and to excise the turgid or difficult passages. One of his followers remarked at the

[1] *Journal*, vol. v, p. 296.
[2] *Letters*, vol. viii, p. 107. Churchey's works are described in chap. viii.

time: 'It is a wonder Mr. Wesley does not abridge the Gospel According to St. John.'

It is interesting next to see him at work on a novel. In 1766, Henry Brooke published his novel, *The Fool of Quality; or The History of Henry, Earl of Moreland*. Henry Brooke had a strong moral purpose in writing this, and was deeply under the influence of mysticism and Jacob Boehme. He was not a Methodist, though his brother Robert and two of his sons were followers of Wesley. Wesley read *The Fool of Quality* and Brooke's later novel, *Juliet Grenville*. He was greatly impressed and thought it 'the most excellent of its kind of any that I have seen in the English or any other language'. Wesley often wrote to his friend Henry Brooke, nephew of the novelist, and on July 8, 1774, he sent him the following letter:

DEAR HARRY,—When I read over in Ireland *The Fool of Quality*, I could not but observe the design of it, to promote the religion of the heart, and that it was well calculated to answer that design; the same thing I observed a week or two ago concerning *Juliet Grenville*. Yet there seemed to me a few passages both in the one and the other which might be altered to the better; I do not mean so much with regard to the sentiments, which are generally very just, as with regard to the structure of the story, which seemed here and there to be not quite clear. I had at first a thought of writing to Mr. Brooke himself, but I did not know whether I might take the liberty. Few authors will thank you for imagining you are able to correct their works. But if he could bear it and thinks it would be of any use, I would give another reading to both these works, and send him my thoughts without reserve, just as they occur.[1]

The young man replied:

He [Henry Brooke, Senior] is deeply sensible of your very kind offer and most cordially embraces it. He has desired me to express the warmth of his gratitude in the strongest terms, and says he most cheerfully yields the volumes you mention to your superior judgement, to *prune*, erase, and alter as you please. He only wishes they could have had your eye before they appeared in public. But it is not yet too late. A second edition will appear to great advantage when they have undergone so kind a revisal. . . .[2]

No other letters about this matter have been found, but apparently Wesley began his abridgement in a leisurely

---

[1] *Letters*, vol. vi, p. 96.
[2] *The Fool of Quality*, by Henry Brooke. Life by E. A. Baker. Library of Early Novelists, Routledge.

manner, for it was not until 1781 that he issued in two volumes, *The History of Henry, Earl of Moreland*. Brooke's original Preface, beginning, 'I hate prefaces. I never read them, and why should I write them?' was omitted, and Wesley put in a new Foreword:

> *To the Reader*. The whimsical title formerly prefixt to this book gave me such a prejudice against it, that I expected to find Nothing in it worth reading. So I just opened it and threw it aside. . . . I was indeed a little disgusted with the spinning out of the story, so as to fill five volumes, and wished some of the digressions had been pared off. . . .
>
> I have omitted, not only all the uninteresting dialogues between the Author and his Friend, but most of the trifling and ludicrous incidents which give little entertainment to men of understanding . . . also a great part of the Mystic Divinity, as it is more philosophical than scriptural.

This was dated March 4, 1780. It was not signed and there was no mention of Wesley throughout the book. There was also no mention of Henry Brooke.

The Wesley edition was popular, and several other editions came out after his death and throughout the first half of the nineteenth century. When the original version is compared with the Wesley edition, it must be admitted that Wesley's methods are seen at their best. The main story, with all the fights and the tears, is retained and most of the long and tedious digressions about mysticism with the moralizations over the incidents of the story are omitted. In many ways it is an excellent edition of the book, and it is tempting to wish that some other novelists had followed Brooke's example and sent along their volumes.

Wesley, however, has often been attacked for re-issuing the book, and it has been asserted that he printed the novel without its author's consent, palming it off as his own work. Charles Kingsley, in his Preface to *The Fool of Quality* in 1859, says that so successful was Wesley that 'country Wesleyans still believe their great prophet to have been himself the author of the book'. The letters given above, however, free Wesley from the charge of pirating and of sending it out as his own work. A more recent editor,

E. A. Baker, says that the novelist Brooke was doting when Wesley wrote to the nephew, who took the matter into his own hands.[1] This, again, is probably unfair. Brooke certainly had periods of madness towards the end of his life, but Wesley's letter was written in 1774 and Brooke died in 1783. In Isaac D'Olier's *Memoirs of the Life of Mr. Henry Brooke*, published in 1816, it is clearly stated that the novelist was quite sane at the time of Wesley's letter. The young man, nephew of the novelist and the subject of D'Olier's Life, was an artist and a Methodist. From all that can be learned he was of irreproachable character, and there seems no reason to think that he lied when he said that his uncle encouraged Wesley to abridge the book. Could more letters be found, the matter might be cleared up; but why Wesley omitted the author's name from his edition remains at present a mystery. This seems to be his only fault in issuing *The History of Henry, Earl of Moreland*.

There are two other publications that ought to be noted in this section, the first being the *Arminian Magazine*. In 1778 Wesley began the *Arminian Magazine, consisting of Extracts and Original Treatises on Universal Redemption*. This was intended to answer the attacks of the Calvinists in the *Gospel Magazine*, and to educate and edify the reader. Each number was to consist of four parts:

First, A defence of that grand Christian doctrine, 'God willeth all men to be saved, and to come to the knowledge of the truth'. Secondly, An extract from the life of some holy man. . . . Thirdly, Accounts and letters containing the experience of pious persons; and, Fourthly, Verses explaining or confirming the capital doctrines we have in view.[2]

The magazine gave Wesley a chance to publish many of his sermons, and to reproduce some of his books that had not secured great sales, owing to their price. He also invited his preachers to submit accounts of their lives, which were published in each month's issue. These form a valuable commentary on the whole movement and are dealt with in a

[1] *The Fool of Quality*, by Henry Brooke. Life by E. A. Baker. Library of Early Novelists, Routledge.
[2] *Arminian Magazine*, 1778, Preface.

later section. Lives of great heroes and churchmen of the past were included, and another section was devoted to accounts of strange and supernatural happenings. These queer tales formed the raw material for several novelists in the next century, and their profound influence on the Brontë sisters and George Eliot has been recently proved.[1]

At the end of each month's magazine were several pages of poetry, some by the Wesleys, but many more by unknown writers. Most of this was of a religious nature, but there were many exceptions, some of which, without showing any great measure of inspiration, can still give pleasure to the reader in sympathy with the eighteenth century.

Later on, more of Charles Wesley's religious poems were included, together with selections from Pope, Dryden, Watts, Cowper, John Newton, Byrom, and many lesser-known writers, as well as translations from Latin verse. These are mixed up with epigrams and verses from tombstones. As the magazine developed, its contents became more varied and many extracts from books were introduced.

He included extracts from his natural science book, *The Wisdom of God in the Creation*, from Locke's *Essay on Human Understanding*, and from books of travel, mixing in accounts of dire, supernatural events and harrowing descriptions of death-beds.[2]

The *Arminian Magazine* was continued after Wesley's death in 1791, but was changed to the *Methodist Magazine* in 1798. In 1822 the title was changed again to the *Wesleyan Methodist Magazine*, only to return at the Methodist Reunion in 1933 to the *Methodist Magazine*, under which title it is published to-day.[3]

---

[1] See *Methodist Good Companions*, by G. E. Harrison, 1935.

[2] Wesley chose as his Editor, Thomas Olivers, whose activities are described in chap. ix, but he himself seems to have decided the contents of the magazine.

[3] The *Arminian Magazine* was vastly superior in every way to the rival *Gospel Magazine*, which was badly printed on cheap paper and is only noteworthy for the violence of its abuse of John Wesley. He is described, amongst other things, as 'this horrid man', 'this prowling wolf', 'this unfeeling and unprincipled flatterer', 'this lyar of the most gigantic magnitude', 'the most unprincipled being that waddles on the surface of the planet'. There was no abuse in the *Arminian Magazine*. After Wesley's death, its stories become more miraculous and strange. Great faith must have been necessary in order to believe half of them.

The last work to be considered in this section is the largest of all Wesley's publications, begun in 1749 and finished in 1755. This was:

A *Christian Library*: Consisting of Extracts from, and Abridgements of, the Choicest Pieces of Practical Divinity which have been published in the English Tongue. In fifty volumes.

As he found time during his travels, Wesley made these abridgements and published them when he could, though generally he only marked the passages in the text he was reading and added simple notes to connect them up. He complained afterwards that the printers often mistook his intentions and left in a hundred passages he had meant to omit. He frequently exhorted his followers to read and study these selections, but the sales were not as great as he had hoped, and he estimated that he lost over £100 in the venture.

In these fifty volumes he included 'all that was most valuable in the English tongue', beginning with the *Epistles of S. Clement, S. Polycarp and S. Ignatius* and summarizing and making extracts of the works of Fox, Bunyan, and Baxter, as well as a host of Puritan and seventeenth- and eighteenth-century divines, 'a multitude of them it would be tedious even to name'. He followed his usual method when he found 'blemishes . . . circumlocutions and repetitions'.

There were many mistakes in the fifty volumes, and Wesley slowly re-read them and made corrections in the copies now in Richmond College. He died before it was finished and the Second Edition appeared between 1819 and 1826 under the editorship of Thomas Jackson.[1]

This completes the examples of the representative publications of Wesley, though a glance through Richard Green's *Bibliography* of his complete works shows the amount that has been left untouched here.

The re-issues of older books and the educational works seem to me to show that Wesley's work at Oxford left a far

---

[1] To Richard Green belongs the credit of reading the whole of the fifty volumes and comparing the extracts and summaries with the original books. In his *Bibliography* he gives details of the amount of shortenings and omissions in each extract.

greater effect on him than has generally been assumed. While he was a Fellow at Lincoln College, he presided daily over the Disputations, heard the various arguments, and then summed-up the proceedings. Before that, as a tutor, he advised on his students' reading and pointed out the important passages in various books. When he came later to his educational and publishing work, he seems simply to have carried over these same processes. He thought he saw a need for a cheap book on a certain subject, so he found the best work on that subject that he knew. He never doubted his own ability to abridge any book in the world, and he considered that most books were improved in this manner. Having marked the most important parts, and possibly starred 'the most sublime passages', he consulted a few other writers on the same matter, just as he would have done in order to prepare a lecture. Next he joined up his extracts, altered a few of the hard words, appended notes taken from the various authorities, added a preface, and published it. His prefaces contain some of his most interesting views as well as his best prose: they generally state the books from which the matter is drawn, but about this he was careless at times.

Examination shows that, with a few exceptions, such as the edition of the *Pilgrim's Progress*, he was conspicuously successful in seizing on the most important points of any book he read, and their many editions prove that they were popular for a long period. His most bitter opponents in the second half of the century were the writers in the Calvinistic *Gospel Magazine*. They poured some scorn on the varied nature of the Wesley books, but reserved their most scathing remarks for the habit of abstracting materials from other books. They accused him of writing nothing himself except the *Journal*, 'a self-important publication which showed his weakness, vanity, and insolence'. It is a pity that he never replied to their attacks on any of his personal affairs; for, had he done so, he might have given some reasons why he failed sometimes to put authors' names to their works.

The *Memoirs of James Lackington*, which are described later, show the growth of the reading public during the century.

This was closely bound up with the growth in cheap and popular literature.[1] Justice in this connexion has not been done to Wesley both for the quantity and the variety of his books, though Richard Green, in the Preface to his *Bibliography*, makes the claim: 'It is Wesley who deserves the credit of having been the first in this country to provide cheap popular literature of a useful kind.' Much research might be necessary to prove whether he was either first or published most in the century, and the point seems unimportant; but his great work in providing books and encouraging reading and study deserves to be acknowledged.

Most of these books now have more interest as literary history or as indications of the social life of the time than as reading for the present. The very nature of their contents makes this so. The history, grammars, natural science, and logic are out of date, like most of the others of the century; the works on medicine and electricity serve only for amusement; the anthologies may be of interest to those in love with minor eighteenth-century verse; there remains, then, the *Arminian Magazine*, with many features of interest and containing the lives of the early preachers. A separate chapter is devoted to these.

When the enormous amount of work and travel accomplished by John Wesley is remembered, and his varied literary productions are considered, in Richard Green's words, 'it cannot fail to excite surprise'.

---

[1] Sir Leslie Stephen has stressed the work of Sir John Hall and of John Campbell, described by Dr. Johnson as 'the richest author who ever grazed the common of literature', who contributed to the *Modern Universal History* and wrote the *Political Survey of Great Britain* and a great number of other works.

THE POETRY OF JOHN AND CHARLES WESLEY

JOHN WESLEY: German Translations. George Herbert. CHARLES WESLEY: Quantity, repetition. Influence of the Bible and other poets. Mysticism. Satire. Arminian influence. 'Spaciousness.' Romanticism. The couplet.

CHAPTER V

THE POETRY OF JOHN AND CHARLES WESLEY

THE poetry of the two brothers has to be considered together because often it is very difficult to tell who wrote an individual poem, and many issues of *Hymns and Sacred Poems* were published as written by John and Charles Wesley without any distinguishing mark. It is known, however, that John made most of the translations and that Charles wrote the large majority of the others. No attempt will be made here to assign all the 6,000 or 7,000 poems to their separate authors, nor shall I try to distinguish between all the different publications and editions.

It is difficult to differentiate between a religious poem and a hymn, and though many of Charles Wesley's metrical compositions were afterwards adapted and verses selected for inclusion in hymn-books published for the Methodists, they were first published in poems written for special occasions, or on topics concerning the state of the country or happenings in the lives of the brothers. The original poems were generally far too long or unsuitable in parts for singing by any congregation. Most of them were connected with religion or with the death of friends, so that they are perhaps best termed 'religious poems'.

First, the translations certainly made by John Wesley ought to be noted.[1] When he set sail for Georgia in 1735, he

---

[1] *The English Poets*, edited by T. H. Ward, vol. iii, contains an account by A. P. Stanley of the poetry of the Wesleys. He is completely unsympathetic to John Wesley as a poet. He speaks of 'men who have hardly a particle of poetic fire in their souls. . . . Amongst such John Wesley is conspicuous. . . . In the prosaic century with which his life was co-extensive he was almost the least qualified to produce a substantial addition to its poetry'. This critic's theological prejudice seems to colour his account too strongly for his attack to be taken seriously. He is kinder towards Charles Wesley, whose 'gifts showed themselves in the closer tenacity with which he clung to the Church of his fathers'.

was struck with the singing of the Germans on board and immediately noted in his diary that he was starting to learn the language. By the end of the three months' voyage he mentioned that he was translating hymns. Thirty-three hymns from the Moravian *Herrnhut Gesangbuch* and some other poems were translated in America or immediately on his return to England. He shows great skill in varying from almost literal translation to the expression of the main thought in verse, which has the great merit certainly of reading as if it had always been in English. Besides the hymns of Pietists and Moravians, he translated some of the classical hymns of Gerhardt, Scheffler, and Tersteegen.

In connexion with John Wesley as a translator, I shall consider his treatment of George Herbert. Herbert was the favourite poet of Wesley's mother, and there are frequent quotations from him in their correspondence, which is the more strange because the metaphysical poets were out of favour during the eighteenth century. Henry Vaughan's poems were not reprinted between his own lifetime and the nineteenth century; Crashaw's poems were not reprinted between 1670 and 1785; and George Herbert's poems were not reprinted between 1709 and 1799. Cowper was one of the few who showed appreciation of Herbert, but even he called his poems 'gothic and uncouth'.

Wesley was greatly attracted by Herbert and probably did more than any other man to keep alive any knowledge of him in that century. His *Journal* and his *Letters* show constant quotations from *The Temple* and *The Country Parson*; forty-eight pages of his anthology, *A Collection of Moral and Sacred Poems*, were taken up with poems of Herbert; Walton's *Life of Herbert* was included in 'A Christian Library'; and in 1773 he issued a separate book, *Select Parts of Mr. Herbert's Sacred Poems*. In addition, he wrote to the *Monthly Review* in 1756 protesting against what he considered to be a slighting reference to Herbert, and said that his poems were 'scarce inferior either in sense or language to most compositions of the present age'.

When he went to Georgia, he quickly felt the need of a hymn-book something like that of the Germans, because there was no provision for hymns in the Church of England service. The Book of Common Prayer recognized anthems and metrical psalms, but the ordinary service of the time had no hymn-singing. Dissenters were beginning to use the hymns of Watts and Dr. Doddridge, and possibly some parsons did use hymns on occasions. Wesley, as I have shown, began to translate hymns from German, then selected some written by Watts, chose verses from the poems of Addison and Samuel Wesley, and issued in 1737 at Charlestown what was probably the first hymn-book printed for use in the Church of England, *A Collection of Psalms and Hymns*. Included in this were six of Herbert's poems adapted from *The Temple*. Later on, he adapted in all forty-seven poems from Herbert.

It was his habit to sing over his translations and adaptations to well-known tunes, which seem chiefly to have been those set to the metrical psalms of Tate and Brady or Sternhold. These were iambic and in three measures, long (8.8.8.8), common (8.6.8.6), and short (6.6.8.6). He changed Herbert's poems to make them fit these measures, to explain the difficult passages, and to make them conform to the taste of the century. To-day much of the charm of Herbert is seen to lie in his use of short lines; but in the Wesley versions these all disappear. For example, in—

> Sweet day, so cool, so calm, so bright,
> The bridall of the earth and skie:
> The dew shall weep thy fall to-night;
> For thou must die,

Wesley was able to keep the first three lines, but altered the last to—

> For Thou and all thy Sweets must die.

Herbert's simplicity, too, did not suit the taste of the century, and sometimes this had to be altered to the 'family language' which they preferred. In *Man's Medley*, Herbert has:

> Heark how the birds do sing
> And woods do ring.

Wesley changes this to:

> Hark how the Woods with Music ring,
> How sweet the Feather'd Minstrels sing!

Though such alterations now seem to spoil the charm of
Herbert, those with a taste for eighteenth-century verse can
find great pleasure in many of the adaptations, and admire
the skill shown in obtaining the smoothness so desirable at
the time. For example, here are two verses from *Grace*:

> My stock lies dead, and no increase
> Does Thy past gifts improve:
> O, let Thy graces without cease
> Drop gently from above. . . .
>
> Death is still digging like a mole
> My grave, where'er I move;
> Let grace work too, and on my soul
> Drop gently from above.[1]

Such adaptations may be considered either wholly or
partially bad, or even allowable and praiseworthy if they
suit the taste of an age, but it seems as if they did not suit
the taste of Wesley as he grew older. In the large hymn-book
of 1779 he only included one of these poems, and in 1773 he
published his selections of Herbert in the original words.[2]

The Poetical Works of John and Charles Wesley occupy thirteen
volumes of about 500 pages each, and those most competent
to judge[3] attribute most of these 6,000 or 7,000 poems to the
younger brother.

This enormous number is obviously not all of the same
merit, though Charles Wesley is not an unequal poet.[4] He
suffers rather from repetition than from any bad verse. The
same ideas are expressed so many times and in so many
different metres that too often a level mediocrity is all that is

---

[1] *Poetical Works*, vol. i, p. 40.

[2] For some points about Wesley and George Herbert, I am indebted to an
article in the *London Quarterly and Holborn Review* for October, 1936, entitled
'John Wesley and George Herbert', by F. E. Hutchinson, Canon of Worcester.

[3] For example, G. Osborn, who edited the poetical works of the Wesleys,
and Thomas Jackson, who wrote the *Life of Charles Wesley*, 1841.

[4] 'They are adapted to almost every situation in social life; they express
nearly every shade of religious feeling; and it is astonishing what a high level
of excellence most of them attain.'—Professor Courthope in *A History of English
Poetry*, vol. v, p. 343.

attained. It is not difficult, however, to show that he often rises above mere metrical ability, and that when moved he rises to the level of the other religious poets of any period in England. In recent years this is beginning to be recognized, and examples of his work have been included in several anthologies. 'He can be virile, felicitous, vivid: if his sweetness often clogs, he has a depth of feeling which frequently brings him within the ranks of the poets.'[1]

Some of his strength and his weakness are closely allied: his poems are often mere rhyming extracts from the Bible. Sometimes one verse of a poem will have seven or eight separate Biblical phrases in its eight lines. For a time this is pleasing, and often the compilation is happy, yet it tends to make continuous reading of his poetry more monotonous. He must have had a particularly retentive memory, because, not only are his poems full of Biblical quotation, but there are very frequent phrases from many other writers. He probably knew by heart much of *Paradise Lost*, as well as the poems of Young and Prior, for phrases from these writers abound in his poems. For an example of his use of Biblical phrases, almost any verse he wrote would serve, though I shall take what is probably his best-known hymn:

> Jesu, Lover of my soul,[a]
>   Let me to Thy Bosom fly,[b]
> While the nearer waters roll,[c]
>   While the tempest still is high:[d]
> Hide me, O my Saviour, hide,[e]
>   Till the storm of life be past;[f]
> Safe into the haven guide;[g]
>   O receive my soul at last.[h]

[a] Wisdom xi. 26: 'But thou sparest all, for they are thine, O Lord, thou lover of souls.'

[b] John xiii. 23: 'Now there was leaning on Jesus' bosom one of his disciples, whom Jesus loved.'

[c] From Prior's *Solomon*:

> We weave the chaplet, and we crown the bowl,
> And smiling see the nearer waters roll.

[d, e] Isaiah xxxii. 2: 'And a man shall be as an hiding place from the wind, and a covert from the tempest.'

[1] *The Cambridge History of English Literature*, by W. H. Hutton, vol. x, p. 360.

f, g, h Psalm cvii. 29–30: 'He maketh the storm a calm, so that the waves thereof are still. Then are they glad because they be quiet; so he bringeth them unto their desired haven.'

A recent interesting study of Charles Wesley's sources has shown his debt to both the Authorized Version and to that of Coverdale—especially the Psalms of the Book of Common Prayer—as well as an occasional word nearer to the Greek than either version.[1]

As an example of his choice of the best-sounding word, there is his use of 'panoply' for 'the whole armour of God', a word also nearer the Greek:

> Stand then in His great might,
> With all His strength endued;
> But take, to arm you for the fight,
> The panoply of God.[2]

The examples of the sources of many of his lines are of interest, but hardly to the purpose here, and I shall but indicate a few of the number from the early Christian writers and from the classics. His debt has been proved to the following: Luther's *Commentary on the Epistle to the Galatians*, Bengel's *Exposition of the Apocalypse*, Ignatius, Tertullian, Æsop, Jerome, Eusebius, Augustine, Plotinus, Plutarch, Dionysius the Areopagite, St. Thomas Aquinas, and Adam of St. Victor.[3]

Among the poets whose phrases reappear in Charles Wesley are Virgil, Horace, Shakespeare, Milton, George Herbert, Dryden, Cowley, Addison, and Pope. It will be sufficient to give only a few examples of phrases borrowed from these poets. A phrase from Milton's *Samson Agonistes*—

> O dark, dark, dark, amid the blaze of noon,
> Irrecoverably dark, total eclipse,
> Without all hope of day!

is used in Wesley's—

[1] *The Hymns of Methodism in their Literary Relations*, by Henry Bett, 1913.
[2] *Poetical Works*, vol. v, p. 40.
[3] For the references to the sources, when they are classical or from theological writers, I am greatly indebted to *The Hymns of Methodism in their Literary Relations*, by Henry Bett, 1913.

> O dark, dark, dark, I still must say
> Amid the blaze of gospel day. .... .

Many examples can be found in *Paradise Lost*, though, for a specimen, here are Eve's words to Adam (book iv, l. 639):

> With thee conversing I forget all time,
> All seasons, and their change,—all please alike.
> Sweet is the breath of morn . . .

Charles Wesley has:

> With Thee conversing, I forget
>   All time, and toil, and care;
> Labour. is rest, and pain is sweet,
>   If Thou, my God, art here.[1]

From Dryden he often borrowed, sometimes taking a whole line, and sometimes merely adopting the form of a poem. For an example of the first, here is a couplet from *The Hind and the Panther*—

> Thy throne is darkness in the abyss of light,
> A blaze of glory that forbids the sight—

in—

> All praise to Him who dwells in bliss,
>   Who made both day and night:
> Whose throne is darkness in the abyss
>   Of uncreated light.[2]

The Dryden song, famous chiefly for its Purcell tune—

> Fairest Isle, all isles excelling,
>   Seat of pleasures and of loves:
> Venus here will choose her dwelling,
>   And forsake her Cyprian groves—

was taken as the base for the hymn:

> Love divine, all loves excelling,
>   Joy of heaven, to earth come down,
> Fix in us Thy humble dwelling,
>   All Thy faithful mercies crown.[3]

It is possibly strange, but it is much easier to find examples of phrases from Dryden than from Pope, though these can be found. John Wesley frequently quoted and expressed

---

[1] *Poetical Works*, vol. i, p. 304.   [2] *Ibid.*, vol. ii, p. 27.
[3] *Ibid.*, vol. iv, p. 219.

admiration for Pope, but Charles must have preferred the
verse of Dryden. This preference was considered one of the
peculiarities of Charles Churchill, another parson poet of
the century. As much more is to be said later of Young and
Prior, examples of the influence of their work will not be
given here.[1] Shakespearean influence is harder to find, and
seems to consist in small phrases, chiefly from *Hamlet*.
There seem some traces of the great soliloquies in lines like
these:

> O what a loathsome hypocrite
> Am I! A child of wrath and sin . . .[2]

and—

> To do, or not to do; to have
> Or not to have, I leave to Thee;
> To be or not to be, I leave:
> Thy only will be done in me.[3]

Enough has probably now been said about the debt to other
poets, but there is generally a pleasure with any poet to
'track his footsteps in the snow', and with Charles Wesley
the footsteps have possibly gone much wider than has been
shown in this account.

An outstanding feature of his poetry is the width of his
psychological description and the penetrating analysis of the
emotional states of a man under differing circumstances.
It is as if the whole of the characters in *The Pilgrim's Progress*
wrote religious poems before, during, and after each adventure; and to these might be added Mr. Badman's descriptions of his feelings. Charles Wesley wrote on the many
different political and national events of his time, received
his chief inspiration from the religious controversies which
beset the Methodist movement, and mixed these with his
own adventures, when going for trial before magistrates,
when acquitted, when accompanying prisoners to Tyburn,
when facing mobs, when returning from riots, when with the
dying, in storms on land and on sea, and when happy in his
own household. But it is the inner state of a man rather than
his outward environment that concerns Wesley, and he

---

[1] Wesley's opinions of various poets is considered in chap. vi.
[2] *Poetical Works*, vol. ii, p. 131. [3] *Ibid.*, vol. v, p. 162.

writes to describe the longings, the prayers, the backslidings, the repentance, the sense of sin, the raptures, the ecstasies, and the peace and joy of the believer. It is this catholicity of interest with the soul of man that gives Charles Wesley his claim to be a poet of distinction.

Of John Wesley, Leslie Stephen wrote: 'Mysticism seemed to him to be simply folly. His feet were on the solid earth: and he preferred the plain light of day to the glooms and the glories loved by more imaginative. writers.'[1] This view of John Wesley is the result of his repeated criticisms of some mystics, particularly Boehme and Swedenborg, and of his concern to keep his followers to the beliefs of the Established Church, with stronger insistence on ethics. Of John the description is not wholly true, but it would be completely false to apply the words to all Methodists or to Charles in particular. In his youth he was strongly influenced by William Law and the German mystics, and later he quoted frequently from Augustine. He brought into English verse the note of *rapture* perhaps more than any other poet. When the Wesleys[2] chose a hymn of Dr. Doddridge for their hymn-books they altered one word in the following verse. It was the word 'pleasure' to the word 'rapture'. Possibly this might be called the keynote of the whole movement:

> Ye humble souls, that seek the Lord,
>   Chase all your fears away:
> And bow with *pleasure* down to see
>   The place where Jesus lay.

This rapture, more allied to mysticism than to the rationalism of much of the eighteenth-century religion, is shown again in the following verses:

> Beyond the bounds of time, and space,
> Look forward to that happy place,
>   The saints' secure abode;
> On faith's strong eagle pinions rise,
> And force your passage to the skies,
>   And scale the mount of God. . . .

[1] *English Thought in the Eighteenth Century*, by Leslie Stephen, vol. ii, p. 411.
[2] I do not know which brother made the change, but possibly they agreed on the alteration. The precise authorship does not alter my argument.

> The Father shining on His throne,
> The glorious co-eternal Son,
>   The Spirit One and Seven,
> Conspire our rapture to complete;
> And lo! we fall before His feet,
>   And silence heightens heaven.
>
> In hope of that ecstatic pause,
> Jesus, we now sustain Thy cross,
>   And at Thy footstool fall,
> Till Thou our hidden life reveal,
> Till Thou our ravish'd spirits fill,
>   And God is all in all.[1]

It is found again in 'For a Preacher of the Gospel', from which two verses are here quoted:

> I cannot see Thy face, and live!
>   Then let me see Thy face, and die:
> Now, Lord, my gasping spirit receive;
>   Give me, on eagle's wings to fly,
> With eagle's eyes on Thee to gaze,
> And plunge into the glorious blaze.
>
> The fullness of my great reward
>   A blest eternity shall be,
> But hast Thou not *on earth* prepared
>   Some better thing than this for me?
> What, but one drop? One transient sight!
> I want a sun, a sea of light.[2]

One of the charges made against Charles Wesley is that he shows too much sentimentality and has an 'excess of sweetness that cloys'. This is more obviously seen from the poor selection of his work included in some present-day hymn-books, where the selectors have chosen those that they think will suit the popular taste, than in the vast mass of his poems. A very few show this fault, in fact, though he has a fondness for certain phrases and metaphors from Biblical incidents that sometimes encourages this view. He had a tendency to speak of men as worms, and to refer to Christ as a 'lovely bleeding Lamb'. He sometimes talked of being 'folded in His embrace' and 'mourning on His dear bosom',

---

[1] *Poetical Works*, vol. v, pp. 168–9. [2] *Ibid.*, vol. v, p. 94.

as well as 'sinking into my earthen bed'. Such phrases, however, occur only in a very small percentage of the poems and
are found far more frequently in the writings of Whitefield,
Toplady, and other Evangelicals. With difficulty, lines and
verses that now seem more amusing than affecting can be
found. For example, a poem on 'The Death of Mrs. Anne
Cowper' has verses with too much literal truth:

> Medicine prolong'd and edged her pains,
> And tore its way through all her veins,
>   And shook her reason from its seat;
> Held on the rack, she *tasted* death,
> And, ground between the lion's teeth,
>   Shriek'd as he show'd the yawning pit.[1]

He wrote many verses to celebrate the defeat of the '45 Rebellion, and it is perhaps difficult to feel all his enthusiasm for
William, Duke of Cumberland:

> 'Twas not the *number* of our hosts,
> That baffled all their furious boasts,
> *Our* wisdom did not cast them down,
> Our courage, Lord, was not *our own*;
> From Thee the sacred ardour came,
> And William breathed an heavenly flame![2]

Throughout the whole of the rebellion he poured out poems
in support of the Government, and, in assurance to King
George that Heaven was aiding him, 'its darling care' and
'its own anointed one'. Several poems were written for the
Public Thanksgiving Day, October 9, 1746, to rejoice that
the rebels were overthrown. The battle was the Lord's, he
said:

> He beckon'd to the savage band,
> And bade them sweep through *half* the land:
> The savage band their terror spread,
> With *Rome* and Satan at their head,
> But, stopp'd by His almighty breath,
> Rush'd back—into the arms of death.[3]

At times there is a 'matter-of-factness' that ought to have

---

[1] *Poetical Works*, vol. iii, p. 177.   [2] *Ibid.*, vol. iv, p. 98.
[3] *Ibid.*, vol. iv, p. 93.

pleased Wordsworth, and he states the moral of a situation with great precision:

> Two are better far than one
>   For counsel, and for fight:
> How can one be warm alone,
>   Or serve his God aright?[1]

Many of his verses for children, however, have been greatly praised and a critic has said: 'In many of *The Graces* written for the young, there is a natural rhythm that suggests Christina Rosetti.'[2] Possibly the best-known children's hymn in the world is:

> Gentle Jesus, meek and mild,
> Look upon a little child.
> Pity my simplicity,
> Suffer me to come to Thee.

An example of the charm and simplicity of *The Graces* is seen in the following quotation:

> O Father of all,
>   Who fillest with good
> The ravens that call
>   On Thee for their food;
> Them ready to perish
>   Thou lov'st to sustain,
> And wilt Thou not cherish
>   The children of men?[3]

A more elaborated one is:

> Glory, love, and praise, and honour
>   For our food
>   Now bestow'd
> Render we the Donor.
> Bounteous God, we now confess Thee;
>   God, who thus
>   Blessest us,
> Meet it is to bless Thee.
>
> Knows the ox his master's stable,
>   And shall we
>   Not know Thee,
> Nourish'd at Thy table?

[1] *Poetical Works*, vol. v, p. 452.
[2] *A Survey of English Literature, 1730–1780*, by Oliver Elton, vol. ii, p. 225.
[3] *Poetical Works*, vol. iii, p. 359.

> Yes, of all good gifts the Giver
> Thee we own,
> Thee alone
> Magnify for ever.[1]

Some of these are reminiscent of Herrick. The influence of the metaphysical poets is strongly marked in many of his opening lines, where he was fond of vivid exclamations or passionate utterance, as if the poem began in the midst of his thought or broke in upon his conversations with the Almighty. A few examples will illustrate this:

> And can it be that I should gain. . . .
> Fluttering soul, what doest thou here? . . .
> O 'tis enough, my God, my God! . . .
> Disconsolate tenant of clay. . . .
> Where is the gourd that sudden rose. . . .

Scattered through all the poems are striking and vivid lines, and the love of music is often clear. 'The best of Charles Wesley's hymns are full of verbal music and easily remembered sound', says Professor Elton. He also points out his fondness for open and ringing vowels, comparing him with Addison. For this might be contrasted the open vowels suggestive of reed-like music of a verse from 'Desiring Death', with the clanging brass of 'The Taking of Jericho':

> As shipwreck'd mariners desire
>   With eager grasp to reach the shore,
> As hirelings long to obtain their hire,
>   And veterans wish their warfare o'er,
> I languish from this earth to flee,
> And gasp for immortality.

> Arise, ye men of war,
>   Prevent the morning ray,
> Prepare, your Captain cries, prepare,
>   Your Captain leads the way:
>   He calls you forth to fight,
>   Where yonder ramparts rise,
> Ramparts of a stupendous height,
>   Ramparts that touch the skies. . . .[2]

This use of vowel music is often combined with strange

[1] *Poetical Works*, vol. iii, p. 364.   [2] *Ibid.*, vol. v, p. 44.

verse arrangements and anapæstic metres to emphasize the triumph or joy of the subject of the poem:

> My Saviour and King,
> Thy conquests I sing;
> Goliath is slain with a stone and a sling.
>
> Thine arm did o'erthrow
> And laid my sin low,
> And now in Thy strength I can tread on the foe.[1]

This metre is found again in 'The Believer':

> In the heavenly Lamb
> Thrice happy I am;
> My heart it doth dance at the sound of Thy name.
>
> True pleasures abound
> In the rapturous sound;
> And whoever hath found it hath paradise found.[2]

There are many attractive verses in *Hymns for the Nativity of Our Lord*, where he seems to catch the true carol note, with something of the apparent simplicity of *The Graces* or the children's verses:

> Go see the King of Glory,
> Discern the heavenly Stranger,
> So poor and mean,
> His court an inn,
> His cradle is a manger:
>
> Who from His Father's bosom,
> But now for us descended,
> Who built the skies,
> On earth He lies,
> With only beasts attended.[3]

Possibly the strongest influence on Charles Wesley came from the controversy between Calvinism and Arminianism which rent the Methodist movement in two parts. Charles Wesley was not only more snobbish but also more openly satirical than his brother, and this note appears repeatedly in his poems. His most biting satire came in 1741, when he crudely stated the Calvinist case in 'The Horrible Decree':

[1] *Poetical Works*, p. 28.   [2] *Ibid.*, vol. v, p. 24.
[3] *Ibid.*, vol. iv, p. 111.

> The righteous God consign'd
>   Them over to their doom,
> And sent the Saviour of mankind
>   To damn them from the womb:
> To damn for falling short
>   Of what they could not do,
> For not believing the report
>   Of that which was not true.
>
> The God of love pass'd by
>   The most of those that fell,
> Ordain'd poor reprobates to die,
>   And forced them into hell.
> He did not do the deed,
>   (Some have more mildly raved,)
> He did not damn them—but decreed
>   They never should be saved.[1]

At that period there were touches of this somewhat bitter satire in most of his verse, but Arminianism was to Charles Wesley—indeed to the whole Methodist movement—something more than the opposite side of Calvinism. It was the dynamic force that gave it life. It was only because they believed that the love of God applied to *all* that their people were prepared to suffer and work, and the Wesleys saw truly that the success of the revival depended on this doctrine. The 'Romantic' elements in Charles Wesley become obvious whenever Arminian views were being expressed. It was when he was feeling deeply about this subject that his words became wild and his verse began to sing. It introduced the feeling of *spaciousness* into his verse.

The idea of size, of great space, of extent, of vast quantity rushes into his verse whenever he is moved, and is his most outstanding characteristic. Water and fire are the metaphors he most frequently uses to express this idea of universal salvation or grace. It is a stream, a river, a sea, an ocean; it is fathomless, abundant, wide, extending, unbounded, unlimited, unceasing, unconfined, inestimable, infinite, exhaustless, plenteous, overflowing, overwhelming, abounding, and never-ceasing; or it is a fire, a spark, a blaze, plentiful, extensive, stretching to the utmost, rising high and higher,

---

[1] *Poetical Works*, vol. iii, p. 34.

giving light to the feast with joy ineffable, bliss-transporting, triumphs, and dazzling raptures. Numbers like 'a thousand', and 'ten thousand', often appear, and the words, 'all', 'every', 'entire', 'plenty' occur repeatedly.

The break from the rigidity and formality of the earlier part of the century and the clearly marked difference from the religious poems of Addison, Dryden, or Pope is easily seen whenever his Arminian feelings are uppermost. This is shown well in the lines quoted by George Eliot:

> Thy goodness and Thy truth to me,
>   To every soul abound,
> A vast unfathomable sea,
>   Where all our thoughts are drowned.

The last verse was—

> Its streams the whole creation reach
>   So plenteous is the store,
> Enough for all, enough for each,
>   Enough for evermore.[1]

It was this lyrical certainty of 'riches unsearchable' to be had in the present life that was the strength of the Methodist movement. They met to sing these songs of joy from the various hymn-books chiefly compiled from Charles Wesley's poems, and it has been well said that 'Methodism was born in song'. In 1779 was issued the *Large Hymn-Book*, which remained the standard book for Methodists for half a century, and its first and last hymns were typical of its whole contents. The first began:

> O for a thousand tongues to sing
>   My great Redeemer's praise. . . .

The last ended:

> Live till the Lord in glory come,
>   And wait His heaven to share:
> He now is fitting up your home:
>   Go on;—we'll meet you there.

Among the 539 hymns there was one about Hell. This 'rapture' is the note that cuts Charles Wesley off

---

[1] *Methodist Hymn-Book*, No. 49. This last verse forms the end of Dinah Morris's sermon in chap. ii of *Adam Bede*.

from the poets of his day and joins him rather to the later Romantics. Probably no other poet between 1700 and 1770 could have written verse of such lyrical happiness as he achieves in a poem like 'On His Birthday':

> Away with my fears!
> The glad morning appears,
> When an heir of salvation was born!
> From Jehovah I came,
> For His glory I am,
> And to Him I with singing return.[1]

Several recent anthologists, recognizing Charles Wesley's value, have included the poem 'Wrestling Jacob' in their books. In this, Jacob's wrestling is taken as the incident to suggest the Divine struggle for the soul rather like the pursuit in 'The Hound of Heaven'. Here is quoted the beginning of the struggle, and the final verse of triumph after the desperate conflict:

> Come, O Thou Traveller unknown,
>   Whom still I hold, but cannot see!
> My company before is gone,
>   And I am left alone with Thee;
> With Thee all night I mean to stay,
> And wrestle till the break of day.
>
> I need not tell Thee who I am,
>   My misery and sin declare;
> Thyself hast called me by my name;
>   Look on Thy hands, and read it there:
> But who, I ask Thee, who art Thou?
> Tell me Thy name, and tell me now.
>
> In vain Thou strugglest to get free;
>   I never will unloose my hold!
> Art Thou the Man that died for me?
>   The secret of Thy love unfold:
> Wrestling, I will not let Thee go,
> Till I Thy name, Thy nature know. . . .
>
> Lame as I am, I take the prey,
>   Hell, earth, and sin, with ease o'ercome;
> I leap for joy, pursue my way,
>   And as a bounding hart fly home,
> Through all eternity to prove,
> Thy nature and Thy name is Love.[2]

[1] *Methodist Hymn-Book*, No. 874.   [2] *Poetical Works*, vol. ii, p. 173.

Professor Courthope, when quoting this poem, said:

It is impossible to read his best verses without recognizing their artistic inspiration. . . . The fact is that the simple fervour of Charles Wesley's religious feelings was always chastened and controlled in the expression by the masculine taste of the scholar and the gentleman, a combination of impulse and judgement which makes him the most admirable *devotional* lyric poet in the English language.[1]

Isaac Watts said 'Wrestling Jacob' was 'worth all the verses he himself had written'.[2]

Wesley's occasional use of the Popean couplet shows ease and ability to employ the most popular form of his age, as, for example, in 'An Elegy on the Death of Robert Jones, Esq.', when he described the life of the household:

> No longer doth their friend like *Dives* fare,
> No *drunken hospitality* is there,
> No revellings that turn the night to day;
> (*Harmless diversions*—from the narrow way!)
> No midnight dance profaned the hallow'd place,
> No voice was heard, but that of prayer and praise.
>
> Not as uncertainly the race he ran,
> He fought the fight, nor spent his strength in vain.
> Foes to the cross, themselves let others spare,
> At random run, and idly beat the air,
> As bondage each Divine command disclaim;
> A truer follower of the bleeding Lamb,
> He bore the burden of his Lord, and died
> A daily death with Jesus crucified.[3]

An example of a complete poem ought to be given, and, though some of his verses of praise for the morning, such as 'Christ, whose glory fills the skies', or poems like 'The Traveller' or 'The Pilgrim' have claims for a place, I will end with a poem in a quieter tone, giving the whole of it. Verses like this make Charles Wesley's place certain amongst the English poets:

[1] *A History of English Poetry*, by W. J. Courthope, vol. v, p. 343.
[2] *The English Poets*, by T. H. Ward, vol. iii, p. 258.
[3] *Poetical Works*, vol. iii, p. 115.

For the Morning

Thou hidden Source of calm repose,
  Thou all-sufficient Love Divine,
My Help, and Refuge from my foes,
  Secure I am, if Thou art mine,
And lo! from sin, and grief, and shame
I hide me, Jesus, in Thy name.

Thy mighty name salvation is,
  And keeps my happy soul above;
Comfort it brings, and power, and peace,
  And joy, and everlasting love:
To me with Thy dear name are given
Pardon, and holiness, and heaven.

Jesu, my all in all Thou art,
  My rest in toil, my ease in pain,
The medicine of my broken heart,
  In war my peace, in loss my gain,
My smile beneath the tyrant's frown,
In shame my glory, and my crown.

In want my plentiful supply,
  In weakness my almighty power,
In bonds my perfect liberty,
  My light in Satan's darkest hour,
In grief my joy unspeakable,
My life in death, my heaven in hell.[1]

[1] *Poetical Works*, vol. v, p. 50.

THE CRITICAL OPINIONS OF JOHN WESLEY

EARLY LITERATURE: The classics. À Kempis. Spenser. SEVEN-
TEENTH-CENTURY LITERATURE: Donne. Cowley. Milton. Dryden.
EIGHTEENTH-CENTURY LITERATURE: *Religious writers:* Watts, Law,
the mystics, Swedenborg, (Jacob Behmen), Byrom. *French Literature:*
Pascal, Voltaire, Rousseau. *Prose Writers:* Walpole, Hume, Sterne,
Chesterfield. *Poets:* Pope, Prior, Young, Thomson, Beattie, Gray,
Mason, *Fingal*, Cowper.

CHAPTER VI

THE CRITICAL OPINIONS OF JOHN WESLEY

THE literary opinions of Wesley have been called by one critic 'an amusing menagerie',[1] though W. E. H. Lecky said that one of the charms of the journals was 'the large amount of shrewd literary criticism they contain'.[2]

Both statements contain a large amount of truth, and an examination of Wesley's works shows that his taste generally conforms to that prevailing in his own time, though he has many striking personal opinions. His letters, *Journal*, and most of his other publications are packed with quotations taken from very wide sources, some of which have not yet been traced.[3] He read many new books as they appeared, and noted down his opinions of them, just as he did of their authors when he met them. In this chapter I shall look at some of his literary views, attempting to keep roughly to their historical order.

I shall not deal with his use of the classics, though it may be noted that Latin quotations abound in his writings, and that he frequently states in his journals and diary that he is reading such works as those of Homer, Virgil, Plato, Horace, Plutarch, Epictetus, Xenophon, Lucian, Cicero, Juvenal, Anacreon, and Demosthenes.

He left Charterhouse with a reputation for writing Latin verse and with a particular love for Horace, whose Odes he is said to have been able to recite. His views on these writers are sometimes coloured by his strong ethical sense, as may be expected, and we find that, after he has read *The Life of Alexander the Great*, by Q. Curtius, he writes:

[1] *Survey of English Literature, 1730–1780*, by O. Elton, vol. ii, p. 221.
[2] *A History of England in the Eighteenth Century*, by W. E. H. Lecky, 1905, vol. iii, p. 121.
[3] See articles in *Proceedings of the Wesley Historical Society*, vol. v.

A fine writer both as to thought and language. But what an hero does he describe! (An account of murders and great slaughters is given.) . . . I doubt whether Judas claims so hot a place in hell as Alexander the Great.[1]

Of the *Meditations of Marcus Antoninus*, he wrote:

What a strange emperor! And what a strange heathen! . . . I make no doubt but this is one of those 'many' who shall come from the east and the west, and sit down with Abraham, Isaac, and Jacob, while the children of the kingdom, nominal Christians, are 'shut out'.[2]

I shall pass over his use of the Christian Fathers, merely noting his wide choice of extracts published in 'A Christian Library'. Throughout his life he was devoted to Thomas à Kempis's *Imitation of Christ*, which greatly influenced him in his youth. His third publication in 1735 was a pocket edition called *The Christian Pattern; or a Treatise of the Imitation of Christ*. This had many changes in the English translation, a Preface, and some advice on reading the book by Wesley. A second edition appeared in 1750, and when speaking or writing to Roman Catholics he always exhorted them to study it, just as he did with his own followers.

He does not refer to many other writers living before 1600, with the exceptions of Shakespeare, Ben Jonson, and Spenser.[3] For Spenser he had a great admiration, and throughout his life he made numerous references to his reading the *Faery Queene*, as well as giving advice to his correspondents to include him in their reading. He only omitted Spenser from his anthology, *A Collection of Moral and Sacred Poems*, because he was 'scarce intelligible to the generality of modern readers'.

From the seventeenth century much more is quoted and there are many references to Jeremy Taylor, Clarendon, Donne, Herbert, Cowley, Waller, Congreve, and, of course, Dryden and Milton. He was fond of quoting from Donne's 'Hymn to God the Father', and in the *Arminian Magazine* for 1779 he included a 'Life of Dr. Donne'. This is Walton's

[1] *Journal*, vol. iii, p. 318.   [2] *Ibid.*, vol. iii, p. 215.
[3] The Methodist attitude to the theatre and drama is examined in chap. ix.

'Life' with a few slight alterations and some omissions. There is no fresh material and no acknowledgement to Walton.

He quoted from Cowley's *Essays*, and defended him from the attacks of 'Mr. Knox', who 'depresses him beyond all reason. He was far from being a mean poet'.[1] There are five quotations in the journals from Congreve, taken from 'Doris', 'The Mourning Bride', and his translations of Horace's Odes.

Milton is the poet most often quoted by Wesley, and I have already considered his edition of *Paradise Lost* and noted his injunctions on preachers to learn off by heart certain passages. He selected passages for the same purpose for Kingswood School, and gave orders that they were to be repeated weekly. He quotes or refers to Milton sixteen times in his sermons, twenty times in his journals, and twenty-three times in his letters. *Paradise Lost* seems to have had most of his affection; for when re-reading the *Odyssey* in 1769 and expressing his surprise at its beauty and value, he said:

> I always imagined it was, like Milton's *Paradise Regained*—
>   'The last faint effort of an expiring muse.'
> But how was I mistaken![2]

In 1763, in the Preface to *An Extract from Milton's Paradise Lost*, he wrote, 'Of all the poems that have hitherto appeared in the world, in whatever age or nation, the preference has generally been given to Milton's *Paradise Lost*'.

The religious poems of the Wesleys show that they were familiar with the works of Dryden, to whom seven references are made in the journals and letters. *Absalom and Achitophel* seems to have been best known. Many of the other poets and writers of the century are casually mentioned by Wesley, but there is little outstanding criticism.

In the first half of the eighteenth century there are a number of religious writers with claims of considerable literary value, and I shall look at these next.

---

[1] *Journal*, vol. vi, p. 292. The book was *Essays Moral and Literary*, by Vicesimus Knox, a parson and writer of many miscellaneous books. Dr. Johnson recommended it to the publisher, and it appeared anonymously in 1778. The second edition in 1779 had the author's name. Cowley is discussed in Essay 169.

[2] *Ibid.*, vol. v, p. 339.

John Wesley sang many of the hymns of Dr. Watts throughout his life, and included a few in most of his hymn-books; but he has not left any observations about them. With his brother Charles, he met Watts at least once in 1738 when they 'walked and sang' together. He read many of his prose works, acknowledged their value, but remained critical of their style and some of the matter. Of Watts's 'Essay on Liberty'[1] he said: 'I was much disappointed. It is abstruse and metaphysical', and though he found many 'just and useful observations' in *The Improvement of the Mind*,[2] he said they were mixed with the 'trite and obvious'. Of this last Dr. Johnson said in his *Life of Watts*: 'Few books have been perused by me with greater pleasure.' Wesley admired Watts's 'Treatise on the Passions',[3] and republished some of it in the *Arminian Magazine* for 1782, with a characteristic comment: 'His hundred and seventy-seven pages will make a useful tract of four and twenty.'

During the century there was a strong revival of interest in mysticism, and many minds were affected, the most important Englishman being William Law, who drew his inspiration through Jacob Behmen[4] (or Böhme). Through admiration for Law as well as general interest in the subject, Wesley tried repeatedly to read of the visions and rhapsodies of the mystics, but generally he was unsatisfied and called for more stress on ethics, on the Bible, and on the Scripture story of Christ. A typical attempt of his to read Behmen is described thus:

Here I met once more with the works of a celebrated author, of whom many great men cannot speak without rapture and the strongest expressions of admiration—I mean Jacob Behmen. . . . I seriously considered what I read, and endeavoured to weigh it in the balance of the sanctuary. And what can I say concerning the part I read? I can and must say thus much (and that with as full evidence as I can say that two and two make four), it is most sublime nonsense, inimitable bombast, fustian not to be paralleled.[5]

[1] *Philosophical Essays*, by Isaac Watts, 1733.
[2] *The Improvement of the Mind*, 1741.
[3] *Philosophical Essays*, by Isaac Watts, 1733.
[4] Jacob Behmen, born in Upper Lusetia in 1575, was a shoemaker. His first work appeared in 1612 and was entitled *Aurora, or the Rising Sun*. He wrote about twenty more mystical books. He died in 1624.
[5] *Journal*, vol. iii, p. 17.

He tried many times also to read the writings of Baron Swedenborg, and sometimes thought he saw certain values, though his usual verdict is well illustrated in these extracts:

He is one of the most ingenious, lively, entertaining madmen that ever set pen to paper. But his waking dreams are so wild, so far remote both from Scripture and common sense, that one might as easily swallow the stories of 'Tom Thumb' or 'Jack the Giant-Killer'.[1]

After reading Swedenborg's *Theologia Cælestis*, he wrote:

It surely contains many excellent things. Yet I cannot but think the fever he had twenty years ago, when he supposes he was 'introduced into the society of angels' really introduced him into the society of lunatics; but there is something noble even in his ravings:

> His mind has not yet lost
> All its original brightness, but appears
> Majestic, though in ruin.[2]

It was in connexion with mysticism that Wesley was critical of the works of his friend, John Byrom. The frequent references in the journals prove their close acquaintance, and notes in the diaries are also found, such as: 'Dined with Dr. Byrom.' In the journal for 1767 he examined Byrom's corrections and emendations of Horace and Homer at some length, and expressed his appreciation of Byrom's own poems. He said: 'He has all the wit and humour of Dr. Swift, together with much more learning, a deep and strong understanding, and, above all, a serious vein of piety.'[3] Much of Byrom's verse was republished in the *Arminian Magazine*.[4]

The mystic writers had a great influence on Henry Brooke, but, as he has already been dealt with in this study, I shall turn finally to William Law. One of the many subjects which connect the Wesleys with Dr. Johnson is *A Serious Call to*

---

[1] *Journal*, vol v, p. 354.
[2] *Ibid.*, vol. v, p. 440. Wesley's rendering of Milton was not improved by thinking about mystics. Here two passages are mixed:
    (i) His form had yet not lost
       All her original brightness, nor appeared
       Less than Archangel ruined (*Paradise Lost*, i, 591–3).
    (ii) Satan is 'Majestic, though in ruin' (*Paradise Lost*, ii, 305).
[3] *Ibid.*, vol. v, p. 517.
[4] When comparing a copy of Byrom's poems with the poetry in the *Arminian Magazine*, I discovered that many of his poems are printed there without any author's name in addition to those which are acknowledged.

a Devout and Holy Life, by William Law. Charles Wesley said that in his youth it altered his whole views and feelings; John Wesley acknowledged it as amongst the stronger influences on his early life, made it a text-book for the highest class at Kingswood, and for some years modelled his preaching on 'Mr. Law's practical treatises'; and Dr. Johnson said:

When at Oxford I took up Law's *Serious Call to a Holy Life*, expecting to find it a dull book (as such books generally are) and perhaps to laugh at it. But I found Law quite an overmatch for me; and this was the first occasion of my thinking in earnest of religion.[1]

As young men, both the Wesleys frequently visited Law at Putney, and were strongly influenced by his views on asceticism, early rising, and the wickedness of the theatre. As he came to believe more strongly in the doctrine of Jacob Behmen, they fell gradually away from him. Letters were written, there were keen arguments, and finally both parties published pamphlets explaining their differences. Law's influence was most strong in Wesley's days at Oxford, and it was not until his return from Georgia that Wesley expressed openly the difference that he had always felt. Thus in 1740 he wrote:

In riding to Bradford, I read over Mr. Law's book on the New Birth: philosophical, speculative, precarious; Behmenish, void, and vain!

Oh what a fall is there![2]

Once again Dr. Johnson would have agreed; for he said:

Law's *Serious Call* is the finest piece of hortatory theology in any language.

But—

Law fell latterly into the reveries of Jacob Behmen whom Law alleged to have been somewhat in the same state with St. Paul, and to have seen *unutterable things*. Were it even so (said Dr. Johnson), Jacob would have resembled St. Paul still more by not attempting to utter them.[3]

But Law's passion and devotion, together with the charm of his literary style, with his clear character sketches, have

[1] Boswell, *Life of Dr. Johnson*, ed. G. Birkbeck Hill, vol. i, p. 68.
[2] *Journal*, vol. ii, p. 297.   [3] *Life of Johnson*, vol. ii, p. 122.

always attracted men of various types who might violently disagree with his views. This has been finely stated by Sir Leslie Stephen, who wrote:

> Perhaps indeed there is a touch of profanity in reading in cold blood a book which throughout palpitated with the deepest emotions of its author, and which has thrilled so many sympathetic spirits. The power can only be adequately felt by readers who can study it on their knees; and those to whom a difference of faith renders that attitude impossible, doubt whether they are not in a position somewhat resembling Mephistopheles in the Cathedral. . . .
> One who has yielded to the fascination (of Law's creed) would alone be qualified fully to explain its secret. And yet no one, however far from Law's mode of conceiving of the universe, would willingly acknowledge that he is insensible to the thoughts interpreted into his unfamiliar dialect. In one sense, not only the Apostles on the Day of Pentecost, but all great movers of mankind, speak a universal tongue.[1]

Although differing from Law about the value of certain mystical writers, Wesley never doubted the worth and beauty of much of Law's own writing, especially when he had, as he thought, extracted the wheat from the chaff. He first did this in 1743, when he issued *Extracts from a Practical Treatise on Christian Perfection*, price 1s. The following year he published a larger edition of *A Serious Call* for 2s.; in 1768 he issued in two volumes *An Extract from Mr. Law's Later Works*; and in 1784 he printed selections from *A Serious Call* with the words, 'Not to be sold, but given away'. He summed-up his views of this last book with the words: 'The *Serious Call* is a treatise which will hardly be excelled if it be equalled, either for beauty of expression, or for depth of thought.'

Leaving the mystic writers and overlooking his reference to theologians, I shall turn to the better-known writers of prose in the century. The diary shows that at Oxford he often read volumes of the *Spectator* and the *Guardian*, as well as Daniel Defoe's *Pyrates*[2] (*Robinson Crusoe*). He makes no comments on these, and has little reference to any novelist in the century, though he seems to have read some novels.

[1] *English Thought in the Eighteenth Century*, vol. ii, p. 38.
[2] The title page of the first edition of *Robinson Crusoe* read: The Life and Strange Surprising Adventures of Robinson Crusoe of York, Mariner . . . with an account of how he was at last strangely deliver'd by *Pyrates*. Wesley may be referring to the *History of the Pirates* which Mr. J. R. Moore has recently attributed to Defoe.

It seems surprising to find criticisms of so many books of travel, histories, and medical books, with constant quotations and comments on poetry of the century, but with no reference at all to Fielding and Richardson. Smollett is mentioned in connexion with his *History of England*, from which Wesley read and quoted. In 1779 he was again reading the book, and noted in his journal what Smollett had said of the Methodists:

. Imposture and fanaticism still hang upon the skirts of religion. Weak minds were seduced by the delusions of a superstition, styled Methodism, raised upon the affectation of superior sanctity, and pretensions to divine illumination. Many thousands were infected with this enthusiasm by the endeavours of a few obscure preachers, such as Whitefield, and the two Wesleys, who found means to lay the whole kingdom under contribution.

Wesley then wrote: 'Poor Dr. Smollett! Thus to transmit to all succeeding generations a whole heap of notorious falsehoods!' After refuting the charges of imposture, fanaticism, enthusiasm, and pretensions to divine illumination, he concluded: 'So does this frontless man, blind and bold, stumble on without the least shadow of truth.'[1] Wesley was reading Swedenborg's *Account of Heaven and Hell* about the same time, so he must have found life particularly irritating. He had, however, a high opinion of Smollett's *History* and used it, together with Goldsmith and Rapin for his own *Concise History of England*. He thought that all historians wrote too much, so used these books as a basis for his own shorter accounts, adding his own interpretations of the lives of Mary Queen of Scots and of Richard III.[2]

In connexion with this King, Wesley mentions Horace Walpole. In 1769 he read Walpole's *Historic Doubts on the Life and Reign of Richard the Third*, which had been published

[1] *Journal*, vol. vi, p. 230. The opinions of Smollett and Walpole about Wesley are given in chap. x. The Smollett quotation is found in *A Continuation of the Complete History of England*, 1764, vol. iv, p. 211. This contains a strong attack on the Moravians in the same chapter as that on Methodists.

[2] Wesley's history appeared in 1776 and was entitled *A Concise History of England from the Earliest Times to the Death of George II*, in four volumes. Goldsmith's history was published in 1771, and entitled *The History of England from the Earliest Times to the Death of George II*. He derived much of his material from Hume. Goldsmith died in 1774 and Smollett in 1771.

the previous year. He found the defence of the King quite satisfactory, and summarized the main arguments in his journal with evident relish.

The only novelist, except Henry Brooke, that Wesley commented upon was Sterne. In his works he casually refers to *Tristram Shandy* but offers no criticism: but in 1769 he came upon Sterne's other famous book and was annoyed by both the title and the contents. He wrote:

> I casually took a volume of what is called *A Sentimental Journey through France and Italy. Sentimental!* What is that? It is not English; he might as well say Continental. It is not sense. . . . For oddity, uncouthness, and unlikeness to all the world beside, I suppose, the writer is without a rival.[1]

About the same time he was reading the letters of both Swift and Chesterfield. He admired Swift's style above all others, but of the matter of the *Letters* he said, 'Was ever such trash palmed upon the world under the name of a great man?'[2] He objected just as strongly to Chesterfield when he read his *Letters*:

> I borrowed here a volume of Lord Chesterfield's *Letters* which I had heard very strongly commended. And what did I learn? That he was a man of much wit, middling sense, and some learning, but as absolutely void of virtue as any Jew, Turk, or heathen that ever lived. . . .[3]

In several sermons he also made critical reference to Chesterfield.

He disliked David Hume's ideas and attacked them a few times in his works. He thought him 'an avowed enemy to God and man, and to all that is sacred and valuable upon earth'.[4] If anything, he was worse than Lord Chesterfield. 'Did Mr. David Hume . . . know the heart of man? No more than a worm or beetle does.'[5]

---

[1] *Journal*, vol. v, p. 445. [2] *Ibid.*, vol. vi, p. 82.
[3] *Ibid.*, vol. vi, p. 80. [4] *Ibid.*, vol. v, p. 458.
[5] 'Sermons', *Works*, vol. viii, p. 342. Hume seems to have said little about Methodism, although he attacked Enthusiasm. In a letter to Rev. Hugh Blair on May 13, 1776, he wrote: 'Two ladies of my acquaintance have laid a scheme of bringing Lady Huntingdon and me together for her or my conversion. I wish I may have spirits to humour this folly!' (*The Letters of David Hume*, ed. J. Y. T. Greig, 1932, vol. ii, p. 524). Nothing more was said about the scheme.

Wesley was far more critical of all prose writers than he was of poets; and of all writers his criticisms are more numerous than his notes of praise. In the *Journal*, quite close to the disapproval of the letters of Swift and Chesterfield, are passages expressing 'great disappointment' in reading Captain Cook's *Voyages*[1] and Sheridan's *Lectures on Elocution*,[2] as well as an attack on Rousseau. Of the poets read during the same period, Byrom, Beattie, and Mason, he defended and admired all.

Hazlitt said, perhaps unfairly, of Wordsworth: 'He condemns all French writers (as well of poetry as prose) in the lump.' John Wesley would have agreed with Wordsworth. He is nowhere more amusing or biased than when he speaks of French literature. For example, he read Pascal's *Thoughts* in 1753 and, though it may be presumed that he liked them, he only noted in the *Journal*: 'I read over Pascal's *Thoughts*. What could possibly induce such a creature as Voltaire to give such an author as this a good word, unless it was that he once wrote a satire?'[3] He proceeded to read Voltaire's *Henriade* and was forced to allow it certain merits, before giving his opinion on French literature as a whole:

He is a very lively writer, of a fine imagination; and allowed, I suppose by all competent judges, to be a perfect master of the French language; and by him I was more than ever convinced that the French is the poorest, meanest language in Europe; and that it is no more comparable to the German or Spanish than a bagpipe is to an organ; and that, with regard to poetry in particular, considering the incorrigible uncouthness of their measure, and their always writing in rhyme (to say nothing of their vile double rhymes, nay, and frequent false rhymes), it is as impossible to write a fine poem in French as to make fine music upon a jew's-harp.[4]

He was prejudiced against both Voltaire and Rousseau and would have agreed with Dr. Johnson when he said: 'It is difficult to settle the proportion of iniquity between them. He [Rousseau] always appeared to me a bad man. That he was mad I never doubted.' Wesley wrote:

[1] *An Account of a Voyage Round the World in the Years 1768-71*, by Lieutenant James Cook, 1773.
[2] *A Course of Lectures on Elocution*, by Thomas Sheridan, 1763.
[3] *Journal*, vol. iv, p. 45. [4] *Ibid.*, vol. iv, p. 188.

I read with much expectation a celebrated book—Rousseau upon Education. But how was I disappointed! Sure a more consummate coxcomb never saw the sun! How amazingly full of himself! Whatever he speaks he pronounces as an oracle! . . .

As to his book, it is whimsical to the last degree; grounded neither upon reason nor experience.[1]

He had formulated his own educational theories, which were certainly not indebted to Rousseau, whom he disliked so much. He turned rather for written inspiration to Locke's *Some Thoughts concerning Education* and to his *Essay concerning Human Understanding*, about which he published some *Remarks*. For educational theory he also looked back to Milton.[2]

Turning to the poets of his own time, we find Wesley far more appreciative. He seems to assume that Pope was the first poet of the age, but, although he quotes his poetry frequently, he gives little direct criticism. Most of the references are those comparing other poets with Pope and pointing out where they fall short of his perfection. For example, when he wrote to Samuel Furly advising him to seek a plain style like that of Swift and to avoid all 'stiffness', he continued by commenting on poetry and saying: 'I was once myself much fonder of Prior than of Pope.' He explained his change of mind, and quoted eight lines from 'An Elegy to the Memory of an Unfortunate Lady'—'Poets themselves must fall like those they sung . . .'—and then added:

Here is style! How clear, how pure, proper, strong! and yet how amazingly easy! This crowns all; no stiffness, no hard words; no *apparent* art, no affectation; all is natural, and therefore consummately beautiful. Go thou and *write* likewise.[3]

Prior is the most quoted poet of the century in Wesley's *Works*, there being in all about thirty quotations. The frequency of Charles Wesley's borrowings from Prior, and his influence on his lines and phrases, has already been described, and it may be recalled that he advised his daughter, Sally, to

---

[1] *Journal*, vol. v, pp. 352, 353.
[2] The best account of Wesley's schools, with their various rules and prescribed books for study, is to be found in *John Wesley and Education*, by A. H. Body, 1936.
[3] *Letters*, vol. iv, p. 257.

learn by heart the first book of *Solomon*. In 1782, John Wesley wrote 'Thoughts on the Character and Writings of Mr. Prior', and published it in the *Arminian Magazine*. This article was occasioned, he said, by the 'particular account' of Prior that a 'Very ingenious Writer' had lately given. The account given by this writer was not accurate, because it was founded on the words of Pope and Spence, who 'depreciated him to exalt themselves'. Wesley never names the writer of the article, but the 'Very ingenious Writer' was Dr. Johnson, and the 'account' that of the *Lives of the Poets*, which appeared in 1781.[1] Possibly it was owing to his friendship and admiration for Johnson that Wesley did not mention his name, contenting himself by attacking his sources: but all the quoted passages are simply extracts from Johnson's *Life*. Johnson is not consistent in his character sketch of Prior, probably because he was joining two or three accounts together. In one place he says:

He lived at a time when the rage of party detected all that it was in any man's interest to hide; and as little ill is heard of Prior, it is certain that not much was known.

Later on he says:

He was not a right good man. He used to bury himself for whole days and nights together with a poor mean creature, and often drank hard. . . . Prior was nothing out of verse and was less fit for business than even Addison, though he prized himself much upon his talents for it.

He said that Chloe, to whom Prior addressed many poems, was probably ideal, 'but the person with whom he cohabited was a despicable drab of the lowest of the species'. Wesley attributed these tales to Pope, and added:

I do not believe one word of this; although I was often in his neighbourhood I never heard a word of it before. It carries no face of probability.

He said that his brother Samuel was a great friend of Prior,

[1] *The Works of the English Poets*, with Prefaces by Samuel Johnson. Sixty-eight volumes appeared between 1779–81. In 1781 the Prefaces were gathered together into four volumes and appeared as *The Lives of the Most Eminent English Poets: With Critical Observations on their Works*, by Samuel Johnson. It was this probably that Wesley read. Johnson obtained much of his materials from the MSS. of Joseph Spence's *Literary Anecdotes*.

as also was Bishop Atterbury, and that these would certainly not have been acquainted with him had he been as this *Life* had described. He continued:

Others say, 'His Chloe was ideal'. I know the contrary. I have heard my eldest brother say, 'Her name was Miss Taylor'; that he knew her well; and that she once came to him (in Dean's Yard, Westminster) purposely to ask his advice. She told him: 'Sir, I know not what to do. Mr. Prior makes large professions of his love; but he never offers me marriage.' My brother advised her to bring the matter to a point at once. She went directly to Mr. Prior and asked him plainly: 'Do you intend to marry me or no?' He said many soft and pretty things; on which she said: 'Sir, in refusing to answer, you *do* answer. I will see you no more.' And she did see him no more to the day of his death. But afterwards she spent many hours standing and weeping at his tomb in Westminster Abbey.

Of *Solomon*, Johnson said:

Prior perceived in it many excellencies, and did not discover that it wanted that without which all others are of small avail—the power of engaging attention and alluring curiosity. . . . The power of tediousness propagates itself. He that is weary the first hour is more weary the second.

Wesley disagreed strongly that *Solomon* was tedious, and said:

Did ever any one discern it before? I should as soon think of tediousness in the second or sixth *Æneid*! So far from it, that if I dip in any of the three books, I scarce know where to leave off.

He continued by quoting about fifty lines from *Solomon* and comparing them with the 'Elegy to the Memory of an Unfortunate Lady'. He found in Prior, 'Ease, Airiness, Lightness, and Facility', quoting for proof the opening lines from 'The Lady's Looking Glass'—lines which he often quoted in his works:

Celia and I the other day
Walked o'er the sandhills to the sea:
The setting sun adorn'd the coast,
His beams entire, his fierceness lost:
And on the surface of the deep
The winds lay only not asleep:
The nymph did like the scene appear
Serenely pleasant, calmly fair:
Soft fell her words, as flew the air.

'Where will you show me any *softer numbers* than these?' asked Wesley. In his works he quoted from many of Prior's poems, including *Solomon*, 'The English Padlock', 'The Garland', 'Earle Robert's Mice', 'Epistle to F. Shepherd', 'Charity', 'Henry and Emma', 'The Ladle', 'Lines to the Hon. Charles Montague', and he has references to 'Sauntering Jack and Idle Joan'. He concluded his review of Prior thus:

> Upon the whole, I cannot but think that the natural understanding of Mr. Prior was far stronger than that of Mr. Pope. . . . And I conceive his poetical abilities at least equal to those either of Pope or Dryden. But as poetry was not his business, but merely the employment of his leisure hours, few of his pieces are so highly finished as most of Mr. Pope's are. But those which he has taken the pains to polish . . . do not yield to anything that has been wrote by Pope, or Dryden, or any English poet, except Milton.

In the *Arminian Magazine* for 1779 he printed Prior's ballad of 'Henry and Emma'. Apparently some readers objected to this, as not being sufficiently religious in tone; for in the Preface to the 1780 magazine, Wesley defended himself:

> It is one of the finest poems in the English tongue, both for sentiment and language; and whoever can read it without tears must have a stupid unfeeling heart.

Thus Wesley would have joined with Cowper and Thackeray in praise of Prior, the latter of whom pointed out his similarity to Horace, 'who was always in his mind'. Wesley's own love of Horace has already been noticed, and possibly he, too, saw these qualities in Prior, for Johnson had remarked that Prior was discovered as a boy studiously reading Horace for pleasure, and then observed: 'The vessel long retains the scent which it first receives.'

Another poet widely read in his own day, both in England and on the Continent, was Edward Young, the author of *Night Thoughts*. Recently it has been described as 'a lamentation in argumentative and reflective monologue, addressed by an actor of superhuman lung power to an audience of still more superhuman endurance',[1] but this hardly does justice to a poet so quoted during the French Revolution—

[1] George Saintsbury in *The Cambridge History of English Literature*, vol. x, p. 141.

on the scaffold by Camille Desmoulins—and admired by Goethe, Burke, and Rossetti, and of whom Johnson said: 'With all his faults he was a man of genius and a poet.' Wesley would have agreed with Johnson, for he saw in *Night Thoughts* 'intrinsic excellence' as well as a 'beneficial tendency'.

As might be expected, Charles Wesley advised his daughter to learn by heart long passages of the poem, and for some reason or other copied the whole of it out several times. John Wesley had published an edition of *Night Thoughts*,[1] and, while acknowledging its faults, was confident that he could remedy them by 'leaving out all the lines that contain childish conceits, that rise into the turgid, the false sublime, or are incurably obscure'. It is certainly a poem that invites such treatment. In his works he quotes— misquotes is the more accurate word—about a dozen times from *Night Thoughts* and a few times from *The Last Day*.

He has a number of interesting short comments on other poets of the time. These are nearly all appreciative. Of Beattie he wrote:

> To-day I read Dr. Beattie's *Poems*; certainly one of the best poets of the age. He wants only the ease and simplicity of Mr. Pope. I know one, and only one, that has it.[2]

Possibly the 'one' was Prior.

Soon after, he was reading Gray's poems, and wrote:

> In the way I read over Mr. Gray's *Works*, and his *Life* wrote by Mr. Mason. He is an admirable poet, not much inferior to either Prior or Pope. . . . I was quite shocked at the contempt with which he more than once speaks of Mr. Mason, one full as ingenious as himself, yea, full as good a poet (as even *Elfrida* shows, as much as Mr. Gray despises, or affects to despise it), and, over and above, possessed of that modesty and humanity wherein Mr. Gray was so greatly deficient.[3]

[1] See chap. iv.
[2] *Journal*, vol. vi, p. 90. Wesley wrote this in December, 1775. *The Minstrel, or the Progress of Genius*, appeared in two parts in 1770 and 1774.
[3] *Ibid.*, vol. vi, p. 134. Wesley wrote this on December 3, 1776. The book he read was *The Poems of Mr. Gray, to which are prefixed Memoirs of his Life and Writings*, by W. Mason, 1775. Modern critics take entirely the opposite view of Mason's garbled version of Gray's letters. 'It is difficult to speak of Mason with justice or moderation', says D. C. Tovey in *The Cambridge History of English Literature*. William Mason's *Elfrida, written on the Model of the Ancient Greek Tragedy*, appeared in 1752, and was acted at Covent Garden in November, 1772. His *Collected Poems* were published in 1764 and 1774.

He refers to Gray once more in connexion with an entirely forgotten writer, when he says:

> I read over a small book, *Poems*, by Miss Whateley, a farmer's daughter. She had little advantage from education, but an astonishing genius. Some of her elegies I think quite equal to Mr. Gray's. If she had had proper helps for a few years I question whether she would not have excelled any female poet that has ever yet appeared in England.[1]

He quoted also from the poems of Dyer (*Grongar Hill*) and was deeply interested in the arguments about *Fingal*. He mentions reading this several times in his journal, at first believing 'the authenticity of it proved beyond all reasonable contradiction' and finding Ossian 'little inferior to Homer or Virgil'.[2] In 1786 he re-read it and noted:

> I was thoroughly convinced it is one of the finest epic poems in the English language. Many of the lines are worthy of Mr. Pope; many of the incidents are deeply pathetic; and the character of Fingal exceeds any in Homer, yea, and Virgil too. . . . Meantime, who is Ewen Cameron? Is it not Dr. Blair?[3]

Thomson had not been included in Wesley's anthology, because he thought little of him. He partly changed his mind in 1772, when he wrote:

> A book was given me to write on, *The Works of Mr. Thomson*, of whose poetical abilities I had always had a very low opinion; but

---

[1] *Journal*, vol. v, p. 252. This book would be *Original Poems on Several Occasions*, by Miss Whateley, printed for R. and J. Dodsley, 1764. It has a dedication to the Hon. Lady Wrottesley, and a very long list of subscribers' names, mostly gentlemen and parsons living in Warwickshire and Oxfordshire. The poems are mildly religious and full of classical allusions. Some are pastorals, and there are many references to 'osiers'. Two quotations may illustrate her style:

> (a) Beneath a spreading osier's friendly shade
>   While bending branches on the waters play'd,
>   Fair Delia sat; the winds forgot to blow
>   And streams to murmur as she breath'd her woe.

> (b) How various is the Female Mind!
>   As with the softest breeze of Wind
>   The trembling osiers move;
>   So, as capricious Fancy reigns,
>   We sigh in Health, we smile at Pains,
>   Admire, despise, and love.

[2] *Ibid.*, vol. v, p. 217. Wesley wrote this in July, 1767. Possibly the book he read was the Third Edition, *The Works of Ossian*, with a dissertation by Blair, two volumes, 1765. James Macpherson first published *Fingal* in 1762.

[3] *Ibid.*, vol. vii, p. 172.

looking into one of his Tragedies, 'Edward and Eleonora', I was agreeably surprised. The sentiments are just and noble; the diction strong, smooth, and elegant, and the plot conducted with the utmost art, and wrought off in a most surprising manner.[1]

Wesley's connexion with Cowper is of interest, if only on account of its slightness. It might be expected that he would have greatly admired his poetry and, since Wesley knew Newton, that he might have met him: but this never happened. In 1758 he met Newton in Liverpool and recorded dining with him once, though he probably met him a large number of times. He thought Newton to be a remarkable man and said that it was a scandal that no bishop would ordain him merely because he had not been to a university. Newton attended Methodist meetings in Liverpool, and spoke for the Methodists with Grimshaw at Haworth. The letters are lost, but it appears that Wesley asked him to become a travelling preacher; for in 1780 Newton's reply was published in the *Arminian Magazine*.[2] Newton continued to correspond with Wesley, and in 1764 was ordained by the Bishop of Lincoln. Wesley read the strange story of his life, *An Authentic Narrative and Account of His Own Experience* (published 1764), and continued to write to him when they differed about Calvinism.

A recent biographer of Cowper,[3] when regretting that belief in Calvinism encouraged his depression, expresses the view that the one man who might have saved him, by stressing the Arminian doctrine, was John Wesley, who might have delivered him from his haunting fears. He has not, however, pointed out how near they were to meeting, which can be discovered by a careful reading of Wesley's letters. A very minor poet and a friend of Cowper was Walter Churchey, who was also a Methodist and frequent

[1] *Journal*, vol. v, p. 485.
[2] *Arminian Magazine*, 1780, pp. 441–4. The letter is dated November 14, 1760. Newton says that he has been preaching for the Methodists at Haworth, but he cannot continue: 'I have not either strength of body or mind sufficient for an itinerant Preacher. . . . To ride an hour in the rain, or more than thirty miles in a day usually discomposes and unfits me for everything. . . . So that though I love the people called Methodists, and vindicate them from unjust aspersions upon all occasions, and suffer the reproach of the world for being one myself, yet it seems not practicable for me to join them farther than I do.'
[3] *William Cowper and the Eighteenth Century*, by Gilbert Thomas, 1935.

correspondent of Wesley. His poems and the letters from
him to both Wesley and Cowper about their publication are
discussed in chapter viii, but it may be noted here that
he thought Wesley might help Cowper. He tried to arrange
a meeting, certainly consulting Wesley and probably asking
Cowper about it. Most of our information, however, has to
come from Wesley's replies.

In 1783 Wesley noted in his diary that he was reading
Cowper's poems, and in 1786 he read *The Task*, which had
appeared during the previous year. He wrote to Churchey:
'I think Mr. Cowper has done as much as is possible to be
done with his lamentable story. I can only wish he had a
better subject.'[1] Two years later they were again discussing
him; for Wesley wrote: 'I am glad you spoke to Mr. Cowper.
What pity is it that such talents as his should be employed in
so useless a manner!'[2] Possibly Churchey discussed a
meeting with Cowper, for a few months later Wesley says in
a letter to him: 'I should be glad to see or hear from Mr.
Cowper; but I have no means of access to him at all.'[3] It is
somewhat ironic that ten days before his death, when he
could not hold a pen to write a whole letter and was only
just able to sign letters written for him by friends, Wesley
should send one more note to Churchey mentioning Cowper.
It was this:

MY DEAR BROTHER,—I have the MSS. I have not seen Mr.
Cowper. Next week I hope to be at Bristol. I am, etc.[4]

In chapter x, Cowper's accounts of the Evangelical
leaders are quoted, and the influence of Methodism on his
work is discussed. In that section also I deal with the whole
connexion between Wesley and Dr. Johnson. Their views
are frequently so similar and deal so often with the same
incidents that it would seem foolish to try to separate the
materials and to give Wesley's account here.

It would be possible, though of little value, to continue to
quote Wesley's opinions about many other minor writers.
A characteristic of all his writing, in journals, letters,

[1] *Letters*, vol. vii, p. 342.   [2] *Ibid.*, vol. viii, p. 74.   [3] *Ibid.*, vol. viii, p. 107.
[4] *Ibid.*, vol. viii, p. 264. Many extracts from Cowper's poems were printed
in the *Arminian Magazine* 1782–9, but the author was not acknowledged.

sermons, and other publications, is his habit of referring to books he had just been reading, quoting or misquoting phrases, and adding some critical remarks. The remarks are incidental to the real matter he had in hand, and though he often has a good phrase or a striking opinion on the writer to whom he refers, he cannot be held up as a consistent literary critic. He seemed to read enormous numbers of books on every kind of topic, yet he never mentions such writers as Fielding and Richardson. When he thought of poetry, he placed Shakespeare and Milton, and possibly Spenser, in a class apart, before he came to Pope and Prior, with whose work he contrasted other poets. He enjoyed many of the poets of his own time, and it must be noted that all his life he constantly read poetry, but his only marked difference from other educated men of his day was his liking for Herbert and some of the metaphysical poets. The religious emphasis probably affected him with these. His taste in verse is well shown in the Preface to the *Hymn-Book* of 1779:

May I be permitted to add a few words with regard to the *poetry?* Then I will speak to those who are judges thereof, with all freedom and unreserve. To these I may say, without offence: 1. In these hymns there is no doggerel; no botches; nothing put in to patch up the rhyme; no feeble expletives. 2. Here is nothing turgid or bombast, on the one hand, or low and creeping, on the other. 3. Here are no *cant* expressions; no words without meaning. Those who impute this to us know not what they say. We talk common sense, both in prose and verse, and use no word but in a fixed and determinate sense. . . .

Lastly, I desire men of taste to judge, (these are the only competent judges,) whether there be not in some of the following hymns the true spirit of poetry, such as cannot be acquired by art and labour, but must be the gift of nature. By labour a man may become a tolerable imitator of Spenser, Shakespeare, or Milton; and may heap together pretty compound epithets, as *pale-eyed, meek-eyed,* and the like; but unless he be *born* a poet, he will never attain the genuine spirit of poetry.[1]

Though this is first of all a defence of his own collection of hymns, it shows also his own standards of taste for poetry. His ideas about prose and his admiration for a plain, familiar

[1] Professor Courthope quotes this Preface and adds: 'John Wesley was fully justified in writing this (*A History of English Poetry,* vol. v, p 343).

style have been discussed before. His taste for restrained and clear writing both in prose and verse was of considerable importance to the Methodist movement,[1] as was also the width of his outlook and his varied reading. His views about individual writers are always interesting and generally vigorously expressed, but it would be foolish to suggest that he was important as a critic. Often he was prejudiced and biased; he knew what he liked, had his own standards, and said immediately what he thought of any new book. French writers, 'infidels', and innovators he condemned in the lump, just as any other proper English gentleman would have done. Despite this prejudice, his tastes were healthy and generally sound. He insisted on good prose from his followers and was 'disappointed' with any writer who fell short of his ideal. In poetry he read Pope and was satisfied.

His views about the numerous books he read add variety and piquancy to all his writings, placing them in a different class from many other religious writers, but his criticism is always incidental to his main work.

[1] The last chapter of this book has a general survey of Methodism and literature, and Wesley's classical tastes are stressed there.

METHODIST AUTOBIOGRAPHY IN THE EIGHTEENTH CENTURY

The *Lives* of the preachers: General account. The education and ability of the early Methodist preacher. Extracts from the *Lives* to illustrate their styles. Childhood. Youth. Conversion. Work. More detail of the *Lives* of Thomas Olivers, the soldiers John Haime and Samson Staniforth, Silas Told, and Thomas Mitchell. The prose of the *Lives*.

CHAPTER VII

METHODIST AUTOBIOGRAPHY IN THE EIGHTEENTH CENTURY

When Wesley died in 1791, there were more than one hundred and thirty thousand enrolled Methodists in England and America, and probably nearly a million adherents. . . . All this had been accomplished in half a century. Never since the apostolic age had there been an evangelistic campaign so rapid, so continuous, so widespread, and so immense in its results.[1]

IT is the intimate account of the lives of the men who achieved this, with their sufferings and fears, their failings and their triumphs that is found in these autobiographies. When Wesley began the *Arminian Magazine* in 1778, he asked many of his older preachers to write accounts of their lives, so that he might include one or part of one in each issue. This was the original source of most of the *Lives*, though they were collected and published in three volumes in 1837, under the title of *The Lives of the Early Methodist Preachers*, edited by Thomas Jackson. About forty *Lives* were given here, all but a few being autobiographies. The two or three biographies are less interesting and written in more official and ponderous English. A few of the early preachers also issued accounts of their adventures and lives separately.

Obviously, there is no common style of writing in these *Lives*, though generally they are written in simple, graphic prose which deserves to be far more widely known. The accounts are full of stories of mobs and the sufferings of simple men for the cause in which they believed, vivid tales

[1] *The Early Methodist Preachers*, by Henry Bett, 1935. This was a lecture delivered to the Wesley Historical Society in 1934.

from soldiers at Dettingen and Fontenoy, moving descriptions of prison and execution scenes, and detailed reports of conditions at sea and of the slave trade that make Smollett's accounts pale in comparison with their realism. Nevertheless, the writers are chiefly concerned with the story of their spiritual development, and often give psychological details of their own early fears, their conversions, and their backslidings. In this they offer comparison with a book to which many of them refer, Bunyan's *Grace Abounding*.

Before attempting a general survey, it is worth dealing in some detail with the assertion so often met with, that these men were entirely uneducated, almost illiterate, but much given to ranting. An examination of 200 who may claim to be the early preachers shows that, with the exception of half a dozen, they sprang from the lower middle class and classes above this; they were tradesmen, farmers, clerks, schoolmasters, or held better positions. Some of them were sprung from families of considerable wealth. There is reason to believe that the middle class, which was smaller then, was much better educated in the eighteenth than in the nineteenth century,[1] and we find that most of these men had been to school till about the age of fourteen and many to the age of eighteen. About one-fifth of them afterwards entered the Church of England or Dissenting Churches as clergymen or ministers.

It is worth examining their education and interests in some detail.[2] Some were learned men. Joseph Benson wrote a Commentary and was one of the soundest Biblical scholars

[1] This generalization might be difficult to prove, but arguments in its favour can be drawn from an examination of many village registers and documents. There were more schools (of the grammar school type) in proportion to the population than in the earlier part of the nineteenth century. Books such as *London in the Eighteenth Century*, by M. D. George, hardly support this view for London, but a good case for its truth in the country is made out by Henry Bett in the books and lectures I have already quoted. I am indebted to him and to a great number of writers in the *Proceedings of the Wesley Historical Society* in writing this chapter.

[2] For this list I have consulted the *Lives* themselves and the obituary reports published in the *Methodist Magazine*. I have not attempted to check the truth of their statements, though most of them have been examined and found correct by writers for the *Wesley Historical Proceedings*. The examples are used to illustrate my main point, that the preachers were not uneducated men, and I have not attempted to state the source of each separate fact.

of his day, while Adam Clarke, who received the Master of Arts and Doctor of Laws degrees from Aberdeen, was the foremost Biblical scholar of the age. Duncan McAllum knew Latin, Greek, Hebrew, and Syriac, and preached both in English and Gaelic. Joseph Sutcliffe was a good Latin, Greek, and Hebrew scholar; he translated Saurin's sermons from the French and published a commentary; he received the Master of Arts degree from Aberdeen. Henry Moore read Latin and Greek authors with Wesley, and later dealt with all his French correspondence and wrote a biography. John Mason was a cultured and learned man, well read in history and medicine, 'and his knowledge of natural history, particularly of botany, was very extensive. In the latter science he was inferior to few in the British Empire. His botanical collections would do credit to the first museum in Europe; and especially his collections of English plants, all gathered, preserved, classified and described by himself'.

James McQuigg was the only man of his day who could read the old Irish manuscripts in the Dublin University Library and was urged to accept a readership at Trinity College. Thomas Walsh was at school till he was nineteen and was an Irish scholar as well as being a prodigy at Biblical Greek and Hebrew. Of him, Wesley said: 'If he was questioned concerning any Hebrew word in the Old, or any Greek word in the New Testament, he would tell, after a little pause, not only how often the one or the other occurred in the Bible, but also what it meant in every place. . . . Such a master of Biblical knowledge I never saw before, and never expect to see again.'

Glancing through the early pages of the *Lives* of the more ordinary preachers, I find these kinds of facts. Alexander Mather was at 'the Latin School' till he ran away to join the Army. John Valton was educated by the Jesuits in France and at a grammar school in England, and was offered £200 a year to become a page to Queen Caroline. John Hosmen and John Floyde became surgeons, and John Whitehead took a degree in medicine at Leyden. John Jones was the author of a Latin grammar and a graduate in medicine and arts. John Hampson had an Oxford degree and published a translation of the *Poetics* of Vida,[1] with learned notes. Francis Asbury was thoroughly proficient in Latin, Greek, and Hebrew, and his Bibles in these languages are still preserved in America, where his travels equalled those of Wesley in England. Alexander Coates spoke Dutch and Danish. Thomas Taylor was educated at a grammar school, and mentions working afterwards in the University Library at Glasgow, as well as employing a Jew to teach him Hebrew. Christopher Hopper 'regarded it a duty which he owed to himself, to God, and to the Church to acquire some knowledge of those languages in which the Scriptures were originally written'; like John Valton, he was a violinist of ability. Andrew Coleman mentions that at the age of fourteen he could recite the *whole* of the *Æneid* and *Paradise Lost*. George Shadford mentions his temptations from reading Ovid's *Metamorphoses* and *Art of Love* when he was a youth. John Pawson was trained for an architect, and was noted for 'his extensive knowledge of the ecclesiastical history of the past age and his deep skill in that of the present'. Of Joseph Cownley, the obituary notice said that there were but 'few books on Divinity in the English language but what he had read'. Thomas Hanson mentions that at the age of nineteen he worked seven or eight hours each day at Latin, Greek, and Mathematics. This continued for four years, and he was helped by two schoolmasters. Thomas Rankin was about to enter the Church of Scotland when he became a Methodist. George Story mentions angling, race-going and theatres in his youth, had a good classical knowledge and, according to Southey, 'tried in early life to imitate the various erudition of Eugene Aram'. John Pritchard, again, was well educated and for a time attended the Academy for Drawing in Dublin. Thomas Meyrick was educated as an attorney. Thomas Olivers came from a wealthy family, became an expert controversialist, and was noted for his talents as 'a writer, a logician, a poet, and a musician'.

Even a potter like Jasper Robinson mentions being at school till he was fifteen.

It would be easy to continue to give particular examples of

[1] Rev. F. F. Bretherton has pointed out many signs of Wesley's deep interest in Vida.

the education of these preachers, but possibly enough has been said to prove the point. It has to be remembered, too, that they were expected to study many hours every day, and some of the books prepared for them have already been discussed. A library was provided at London, Bristol, and Newcastle-on-Tyne for their use, and Wesley often made grants to them for books, as well as taking some of them to his school at Kingswood for special training. It is only when the preachers were recognized as educated men that many of Wesley's rules became sense and the *Large Minutes* can be understood:

> I will give each of you, as fast as you will read them, books to the value of five pounds. And I desire the Assistants would take care that all the large Societies provide our Works . . . for the use of the Preachers.

The *Minutes of Conference* for 1744 gives the list of books that his preachers were expected to study as the following:

> Sallust, Cæsar, Tully, Erasmus, Castellio, Terence, Virgil, Horace, Vida, Buchanan, the Greek Testament, Epictetus, Plato, Ignatius, Ephraem Syrus, Homer, the Greek Epigrams, Dupont, Bishop Ussher's Sermons, Arndt, Boehm, Nelson, Pascal, Francke, R. Gell, our tracts.

There were probably many ignorant men who spoke and preached without authority in different parts of the country and many local preachers who had little education, but the full-time travelling preachers, who carried through the whole revival, were men of education and ability.

So much for the type[1] of men who were the early preachers

---

[1] In 1908 Dr. A. Caldecott, Professor of Moral Philosophy at King's College, London, read an essay before the Aristotelian Society on the philosophic and psychological importance of these *Lives*. It was afterwards published as *The Religious Sentiment, illustrated from the Lives of Wesley's Helpers*, by Rev. A. Caldecott, D.D., D.Litt., 1909. He examined thirty-four *Lives* in detail, and his unbiased verdict carries weight. Of the preachers he says: 'At the outset, let me say that, though these young men describe unusually intense emotionability, they were not of ill-balanced nervous systems; they all lived vigorously, and most of them continued laborious pursuits until advanced old age; they were not fretting under disappointments, or depressed with the *ennui* of prematurely worn-out single emotions, the "sorrows of youth"; nor were they of melancholy temperament, apt to cherish sadness and gloom, averse to cheerfulness and joy; they struggled against the sadness they experienced in the first stage they describe, with an irresistible conviction that it need not be there if only joy could be obtained' (p. 8).

and wrote the autobiographies. Turning to their writings, I shall make a general survey before examining a few in detail.

The *Lives* all begin with the place of birth of the writer and generally add something about the parents, much like the beginning of many autobiographical novels. John Allen starts thus:

> I was born at Chapel-in-the-Frith, Derbyshire, in June, 1737. My parents were honest labouring people, and brought up eight children, all yet living; most of them convinced of sin, and some converted to God.[1]

William Ashman describes his mother:

> She always rose early, never used tea, had five children, was diligent in business, and it never cost her twenty shillings for medicines in her whole life.[2]

The most striking thing about these many accounts is the constant reference to fear in their childhood. Most of them, all through their youth, went continually in dread of the Devil and of Hell. It was generally this fear that drove them to seek out the Methodists eventually. It is the more interesting because they sprang from so many classes of society and from so many differing shades of religious belief. Possibly this haunting of fear had persisted in the middle and lower classes from the Middle Ages. The same thing is carefully described in Bunyan's *Grace Abounding*. His sins in his childhood, and his desperate wickedness, his games and then terrifying fears that the Devil was near, are repeated again and again in these *Lives*. A quotation from Bunyan will serve for comparison on this and on many other points:

> Being filled with all unrighteousness: the which did also so strongly work and put forth itself, both in my heart and life, and that from a child, that I had but few equals, especially considering my years, which were tender, being few, both for cursing, swearing, lying, and blaspheming the holy name of God.
>
> Yea, so settled was I and rooted in these things, that they became as a second nature to me; the which, as I also have with soberness

---

[1] *The Lives of Early Methodist Preachers*, ed. Thomas Jackson, 1837, vol. iii, p. 437. (This edition will be mentioned as *Lives* in the rest of this chapter.)
[2] *Lives*, vol. iii, p. 226.

considered since, did so offend the Lord, that even in my childhood he did scare and affright me with fearful dreams, and did terrify me with dreadful visions; for often, after I had spent this and the other day in sin, I have in my bed been greatly afflicted, while asleep, with the apprehension of devils and wicked spirits, who still, as I then thought, laboured to draw me away with them, of which I could never be rid. . . .[1]

In the *Lives*, most of the writers thought they were wicked as children. The precise Thomas Olivers, who later pointed out the moral of all his adventures, simply says:

I was generally reckoned the worst boy who had been in those parts for the last twenty or thirty years.[2]

A Cornishman, Richard Rodda, seems to have been in the midst of the supernatural from childhood; he had hair-breadth escapes from death in mines, from horses galloping over him, and from great stones which fell around him. In addition, Satan was always attacking him with 'levity'. He describes his terrors as a child:

One time in particular, I was in such trouble that I thought God was frowning over me, and that hell moved from beneath to meet me. Once, a very wicked boy being in company with me, as I walked the road, I was constrained to fall on my knees, and cry aloud for mercy; for every step I took, I feared I should drop into everlasting burnings.[3]

Often, some of these fears seemed to depart and the youth went off to begin to earn his living. Then the fears returned to him, and he was overwhelmed with a sense of guilt and wickedness, though he tried to ward them off by leading a wild and adventurous life. Some, however, did lead a more normal life. For example, George Shadford, after being chased by a parson for Sabbath-breaking, and entertaining his friends by reading Ovid's *Art of Love* to them, notes:

I was fond of wrestling, running, leaping, football, dancing, and such like sports; and I gloried in them, because I could excel most in the town and parish. At the age of twenty I was so active that I seemed a compound of life and fire, and had such a flow of animal spirits, that I was never in my element, but when employed in such kind of sports.[4]

[1] *Grace Abounding*, Everyman Edition, p. 8.
[2] *Lives*, vol. i, p. 196.　[3] *Ibid.*, vol. ii, p. 118.　[4] *Ibid.*, vol. iii, p. 178.

Nevertheless, he was tempted to drown himself and to throw himself over galleries in churches before he ran away to join the Army.

Generally a crisis approached and the writers tell how they tried to find peace. Some ran nearly mad with their sense of sin, and sought remedies in all directions. The descriptions of their sufferings under this conviction of sin are again like those of Bunyan. All this happened before they had anything to do with Methodists. This seems important, because it is often loosely stated that the Methodists came and frightened otherwise happy and contented people. Of course, it has to be remembered that these were accounts written long afterwards by writers who were then settled Methodists and wished to emphasize their present happy state in contrast with former worldly unhappiness. Nevertheless, the constant repetition in these *Lives* of accounts of terror in the writer's youth cannot be overlooked or be fairly attributed to Methodist preaching.

Finally, the sufferers sought out the Methodists with some trepidation, or were taken by friends to hear Wesley or another preach. The crisis came and after a struggle a complete peace was found. Then follows a lyrical description of the happiness, and sometimes ecstasy, which fell on them. Bunyan, too, has this; but he suffers even more afterwards from doubts and backslidings. Sometimes the Methodists suffered like this, but their accounts have far more about their joy and rapture than he has.

Here is the account of John Furz, who rushed out of church in tears:

The people came about me and asked me why I wept. I said, 'I shall go to hell; for I do not believe'. They answered, 'Young man, if you go to hell, no one in the town will go to heaven'.

He dropped senseless with fear before finally meeting the Methodists and being converted.

I that before was dead in trespasses and sins was now made alive to God. I sat in heavenly places with Christ Jesus. I was as in a new world. If I walked out into the open field, everything showed forth the glory of God. If I looked at the sun, my heart said, 'My God made this, not for himself, but us'. If I looked on the grass, the corn, the trees, I could not but stand and adore the goodness of God. . . . And oh, how I longed for all the world to know what I knew![1]

For another example, here is John Pritchard:

My wilderness soul became a pleasant field, and my desert heart like the garden of the Lord; the promises flowed in upon me. I found in consequence of this great tenderness of mind, and much peace and joy through believing. . . . My every meal was a kind of sacrament: the food I ate was life to my soul as well as marrow to my bones. I found a double sweetness in all I possessed. . . . I was now united to a happy people, who walked (the general part of them) in the light of God's countenance. . . . We had a heaven among us and a paradise within us. . . . While I was there, my heart was drawn out in prayer for the whole world. My soul grasped the habitable globe.[2]

Pritchard is one of the more mystical of the preachers, though a great many use nearly the same language. It was their excess of joy[3] that drew others to investigate, and again and again appear phrases like 'We were so happy that we knew not how to part', and 'I was supported with an uncommon degree of cheerfulness'.

After some time of testing and study, they began to speak in the classes and at local meetings. Then came the invitation from Wesley to become travelling preachers, and they give an account of their nervousness or attempts to evade the issue. Some of these are amusing, as is that of the simple and little-educated Thomas Mitchell:

When the time came, my soul was bowed down within me; my bones shaked, and one knee smote against the other. I had many

---

[1] *Lives*, vol. ii, pp. 328, 333.   [2] *Ibid.*, vol. iii, pp. 454–8.

[3] In *The Religious Sentiment*, 1909, Dr. Caldecott stresses this joy and mysticism which appear so repeatedly at this stage of the *Lives*. He writes, quoting Thomas Hanson's words, ' "My heart, with a kind, sweet struggle melted into the hands of God", says not a mediæval Spaniard but a Yorkshire clothier of the eighteenth century' (p. 12). At the end of his essay, he again stresses the importance of the joy they discovered. 'It was not always secured at the outset by any means, and great perplexity and trouble vexed them because of its delaying. In different degrees, some speak of "ecstasies" of joyfulness; while some were regarded by their friends as serious men, but none as melancholy: "sober but not sad", is said of one. They were not like Butler or Johnson or the father of Carlyle—"Man's face he did not fear; but God he always feared" —but men of cheer and happiness, in the expression of which lay much of their attractive power. . . . The simplest explanation of its presence is that it corresponds to the health of the whole mental nature' (p. 25).

to hear me: some of them heard with pain, as my gifts were very small, and advised me to speak no more in public.[1]

Thomas Hanson has an interesting account also:

Not long after this, a letter came from Mr. Thomas Olivers to let me know that I was appointed by the Conference to travel in the then York Circuit. This was done wholly without my knowledge. No one had spoken to me about it, nor I to any one. I already preached four or five times a week about home, and loved the people too well to desire to leave them. In my answer to Mr. Olivers, I said, 'I have no doubt of my call to preach; but have no desire to be a Travelling Preacher. I am not fit for it. I cannot come'.

He replied, 'If your father was dead, and your mother lay a-dying, you must come and preach the gospel'. I wept a fortnight about it. I said to my brother, 'Go you: you are more fit than I am'. He said, 'God knows who is fit. He has called you: therefore go'. . . . I went in 1760. . . . I have been in most of the Circuits in the kingdom. . . .

I have been in dangers by snow drifts, by land floods, by falls from my horse, and by persecution; I have been in sickness, cold, pain, weakness, and weariness often; in joyful comforts often; I have had abundance of trials, with my heart, with my understanding and judgement, with various reasonings among friends and foes, with men and devils, and most with myself. But in all these, God in mercy has hitherto so kept me that I believe none can with justice lay any single immoral act to my charge, since the day when God through Christ forgave my sins. . . .

I have from my beginning thought myself the poor man's Preacher; having nothing of politeness in my language, address, or anything else. I am but a brown bread Preacher, that seeks to help all I can to heaven, in the best manner I can.[2]

Wesley need surely have made few apologies for a follower who could write such English as this.

There are fascinating pictures of the homely details of their lives, their illnesses, and the troubles over their horses. Thomas Olivers gives a gruesome account of an attack of smallpox, and naturally draws the moral clearly:

From this account we learn, first, that none ought to give or take any thing heating, in the beginning of this disorder. Secondly, that while there is life, none ought to despair of recovering, however ill they are. Thirdly . . .

---

[1] *Lives*, vol. i, p. 70.   [2] *Ibid.*, vol. iii, p. 280.

Later he met a farmer and bought a horse for £5:

> We struck a bargain at once, and in a few days I mounted my
> horse, and have kept him to this day, which is about twenty-five
> years. On him I have travelled, comfortably, not less than a hundred
> thousand miles in preaching the Gospel.[1]

There is an amusing account of John Furz being taken ill and
being looked after by the women of a society:

> Many years ago when I was at Hornby, in Yorkshire, I had a
> violent illness. None about me expected that I should ever recover.
> When to all appearance I was near death, Mr. Olivers sent a letter
> to inform me that he would come and preach my funeral sermon,
> and rejoice over me. The good women that sat around my bed
> said, 'We never had a Preacher died here before. We shall have a
> great company of people to hear the funeral sermon'. I heard one
> of them say, 'Now he is going'. Meantime the cry of my heart was,
> 'Lord sanctify me now or never'. . . . And from that instant I began
> to recover.[2]

Here again there is an economy in words that would do
credit to a great writer, and pages of description could
hardly better depict the set of gossipy women that love to
hang around death-beds in country places.

Having given a sketch of the general careers of these
preachers, I shall examine a few in more detail, and for
examples choose the learned and precise Thomas Olivers,
the soldiers, John Haime and Sampson Staniforth, Thomas
Mitchell, with his sufferings from the mobs, and lastly, the
almost unbelievable adventures of Silas Told.

I have already quoted some of the early adventures of
Thomas Olivers, a well-educated man whose poetry is
described in chapter ix. He is most amusing when explaining solemnly how he methodized each situation, and then
drew the moral from it. Not for him the bravado of martyr-
dom or any tempestuous escapes from danger in mobs; he
kept his head and retired with caution. He and his companion were stoned in Yarmouth:

> My fellow traveller galloped out of the town as fast as he was
> able; but I watched the motions of the sticks and stones which were
> likely to hit me, so as to preserve a regular retreat.[3]

[1] *Lives*, vol. i, pp. 214, 221. [2] *Ibid.*, vol. ii, p. 352. [3] *Ibid.*, vol. i, p. 225.

The 'high-water mark' of his *Life* is the description of his choice of a wife, guided as he was so clearly by reason:

My first inquiry was, 'Am I called to marry at this time?' Here I weighed the reasons on both sides, and then concluded in the affirmative. I then inquired, 'What sort of person ought I to marry?' . . . Such a one as Christ would choose for me. . . . 'But what sort of a person have I reason to believe He would choose for me?' [He ranged her properties in order of importance.] The first was grace. I was quite certain that no Preacher of God's word ought on any consideration, to marry one who is not eminently gracious.

The second that she ought to have tolerably good common sense. A Methodist Preacher, in particular, who travels into all parts, and sees such a variety of company, I believed, ought not to take a fool with him.

Thirdly, as I knew the natural warmth of my own temper, I concluded that a wise and gracious God would not choose a companion for me who would throw oil, but rather water, upon the fire.

Fourthly, I judged that, as I was connected with poor people, the will of God was that whoever I married should have a small competency, to prevent my making the Gospel chargeable to any.

Having proceeded thus far, my next inquiry was, 'But who is the person in whom these properties are thus found in the most eminent degree?'

I immediately turned my eyes to Miss Green, a person of a good family, and noted through all the north of England for her extraordinary piety. I therefore opened my mind to her; and after consulting Mr. Wesley we were married.

As in this affair I consulted reason and the will of God so impartially, I have had abundant reason to be thankful ever since.[1]

Defoe might well have been his tutor in writing English.

Next there are the two soldiers, John Haime and Sampson Staniforth. Extracts about the youth of the former have already been given. While in the Army, he heard Charles Wesley and became a Methodist, and afterwards in Flanders, in 1742, he organized meetings amongst the soldiers and formed a little society of Methodists.

Staniforth had a lurid career. His boyhood was rough and finally he joined the Army. An account follows of his seduction of a girl in the Highlands and the attempts of her brothers to kill him. From Scotland he went to Flanders, where he was nearly caught and hanged for desertion and

[1] *Lives*, vol. i, pp. 226–7.

looting before he ran off with the wife of a negro. Finally, a friend took him to hear the Methodist, John Haime. His conversion is vividly described: 'I was as it were knocked down like an ox.' Immediately afterwards occurred the incident quoted by Matthew Arnold in *St. Paul and Protestantism*,[1] and compared by him with that of the Apostle on the Damascus road. Staniforth was on sentry duty at night:

> I saw the clouds open exceeding bright, and I saw Jesus hanging on the cross. At the same moment these words were applied to my heart, 'Thy sins are forgiven thee'. My chains fell off; my heart was free. All guilt was gone, and my soul was filled with unutterable peace. 'I loved God and all mankind, and the fear of death and hell was vanished away. I was filled with wonder and astonishment.[2]

The descriptions of the battles are vivid in the extreme, reminiscent at times of the old ballads and the Battle of Maldon. The whole is worthy of quotation, but some idea can be obtained from extracts. Haime at Dettingen says:

> I had no sooner joined the regiment than my left-hand man was shot dead. I cried to God and said, 'In Thee have I trusted, let me never be confounded'. My heart was filled with love, peace, and joy more than tongue can express. I was in a new world. [After the battle and in the midst of dead and dying.] So, being very wet and much fatigued, I wrapped myself up in my cloak, and lay down and fell asleep. And though it still rained upon me, and the water ran under me, I had as sweet a night's rest as ever I had in my life.[3]

General Ponsonby gave him permission to hold Methodist meetings, and the Duke of Cumberland once attended. Later there were 300 men who might be called Methodists and six preachers with this army. In April, 1745, they came to Fontenoy. Staniforth says:

> When I came into the ranks, I felt some fear, but as we came near the French army, we halted a little. I then stepped out of the line,

[1] *St. Paul and Protestantism*, by Matthew Arnold, 1870, pp. 114–15: 'Paul's conversion is for science an event of precisely the same nature as the conversions of which the history of Methodism relates so many. . . . The conversion of Paul is in itself an incident of precisely the same order as the conversion of Sampson Staniforth, a Methodist soldier in the campaign of Fontenoy. . . . Not the narrative, in the Acts, of Paul's journey to Damascus, could more convince us of its own honesty.'
[2] *Lives*, vol. ii, p. 160.
[3] *Ibid.*, vol. i, p. 160.

threw. myself on the ground, and prayed that God would deliver
me from all fear, and enable me to behave as a Christian and good
soldier. Glory be to God! He heard my cry and took away all my
fear. I came into the ranks again and had both peace and joy in
the Holy Ghost. . . . All the day I was in great spirits, and as composed in my mind as if I had been hearing a sermon. I neither
desired life nor death, but was entirely happy in God. . . . One was
saying, 'Oh, how happy I am!' and just as he spoke a cannon-shot
came and took off his head. We lost four Preachers, and many of
the society.[1]

Haime has a long account of the battle, in the course of
which he says:

When W. Clements had his arm broken by a musket ball, they
would have carried him out of the battle: but he said, 'No; I have
an arm left to hold my sword. I will not go yet'. When a second
shot broke his other arm, he said, 'I am as happy as I can be out
of paradise'.

John Evans, having both his legs taken off by a cannon ball, was
laid across a cannon to die: where, as long as he could speak, he
was praising God with joyful lips.[2]

He gives many other accounts of scenes in the Army abroad
and after the return to deal with the '45 Rebellion, and he
discusses what he considers to be the bad leadership. After
suffering great hardships, he secured his release from the
Army.

The most exciting and the longest story of a Methodist
preacher is not included in the ordinary list of the *Lives*,
though extracts were reprinted in the *Arminian Magazine*. It
was published separately in 1786, and was entitled: *An
Account of the Life and Dealings of God with Silas Told*. This is
about the length of an ordinary novel, and for graphic
incidents and realistic details equals the novels of Captain
Marryat and Smollett combined, with portions of the
Newgate Calendar added. It seems difficult to believe that
it can be true; but John Wesley and others vouch for Told's
truthfulness, references to his work are given in the *Public
Advertiser*, and Hogarth included him in a drawing.[3]

The first part of his adventures was at sea. He was pressed
on board a warship, he was shipwrecked several times and

[1] *Lives*, vol. ii, pp. 163–6.   [2] *Ibid.*, vol. i, pp. 168–9.   [3] See later.

spent weeks on a desert island, he was captured by Spanish pirates, and he helped to stop a mutiny. He spent some years, like John Newton, on board a slave trader around the coasts of Africa and America; he was nearly flogged to death himself and saw negroes killed by flogging. He had to help throw the dead negroes overboard each morning, and watched a captain use their bodies as bait for sharks. An account of the cruelty of some of these captains is unequalled in horror in any book of the century. Like Swift and Defoe, he gives the most exact details and the numbers and measurements and dates of almost everything he describes.

During his career, he heard Wesley preach, and he gives a vivid account of the sermon. He was converted and his friends exclaimed in surprise, 'What! Told, are you commenced a Whitefieldite?' Later, as he was a man of some education, Wesley appointed him to teach at his Charity School at the Foundry. He had sixty boys and six girls there and seems to have been a great success, for he says, 'I continued in the school seven years and three months and discharged 275 boys, most of them to capital trades'. Possibly he was the most exciting school-teacher that there has ever been.

Among other claims to notice, he has that of having seen the legendary country of Hy-Brasil, which numerous people claim to have seen off the West of Ireland. Possibly there is some kind of mirage there at times. Told says that the sailors saw land a few miles off, and could clearly discern green fields and white surf on the rocks so that preparations were begun for landing. The land remained in sight from seven in the morning till six at night. Then—

as the sun was shining clear from the westward, in less than a minute we lost all sight of the land; nothing but the horizon, interspersed with a few pale clouds, was perceptible from the deck. This filled the ship's company with the utmost astonishment; nor did we make the coast of Ireland for several days after. Our captain and the ship's company concluded that it was Old Brazille, which navigators affirm to have been destroyed by an earthquake between five and six hundred years ago.

In 1744, he heard Wesley preach at the Foundry on the

text, 'I was sick and in prison, and ye visited me'. After this he joined Sarah Peters and began to visit Newgate Prison. The terrible account of her visits is given in Wesley's *Journal*. He devoted the rest of his life to work amongst these men and the book becomes a kind of Newgate Calendar of repentances and executions. The story of the groups of men, women, and even children taken every six weeks to Tyburn is still harrowing to read. Sometimes as many as twenty were taken off at a time, and one or two would be reprieved at the gallows' foot, while others fainted and had to be revived before hanging. Many were 'converted' in the days before execution and went to Tyburn singing and apparently happy. Throughout the book are numerous passages like the following:

> In the cart was a youth of nineteen years of age. I said to him, 'My dear, are you afraid to die?' He replied, 'No, sir, really I am not'.

And:

> At the gallows Lancaster prayed extemporary in a very excellent manner, and the others behaved with great discretion.

Sometimes things were not so well ordered and the mob was restless. Then he notes: 'They were turned off in the utmost hurry and confusion.' There is also a strange account of some ruffians, who were paid to steal the bodies from the gallows for the surgeons, being chased by sailors and the body being discovered on the mother's door-step.

When the Ordinary of Newgate resigned in 1773, the Lord Mayor recommended that Silas Told should be appointed to the post, because, says the *Public Advertiser* for October 20, 1773, 'for above twenty years the said Told has repeatedly of his own accord gone in the cart with the condemned prisoners to Tyburn to sing and pray with them'. Hogarth has a picture, 'The March to Tyburn', and the grave-looking man with an open book preaching or reading in the cart is said to be Silas Told.[1] He died in 1779.

---

[1] *A New History of Methodism*, Ed. W. J. Townsend, H. B. Workman, and G. Eayrs, 1909. Vol. i, p. 312, reproduces the Hogarth print under the title of 'Silas Told Preaching to a Felon on the Way to Tyburn'.

Thomas Mitchell lived a life in almost complete contrast, though during the Rebellion he enlisted in the Yorkshire Blues. Afterwards he heard the famous Grimshaw of Haworth and John Nelson preach, and became a Methodist. The simplicity of his *Life* is its chief attraction, and possibly it was his obvious sincerity and childlikeness that attracted Dr. Lettsom, who liked him so well that he attended him without fee or reward towards the end of his life. Wesley wrote to Alexander Mather when he was about to become a travelling preacher and warned him:

> To be a Methodist Preacher is not the way to ease, honour, pleasure, or profit. It is a life of much labour and reproach. They often fare hard, often are in want. They are liable to be stoned, beaten, and abused in various manners. Consider this before you engage in so uncomfortable a way of life.[1]

Nowhere is the story told better, more movingly, or with more restraint than in the account of Thomas Mitchell. The passage where he was advised 'to preach no more' has already been quoted. Next he tells of the district into which he was sent:

> One evening, while William Darney was preaching, the Curate of Guiseley came at the head of a large mob, who threw eggs in his face, pulled him down, dragged him out of the house on the ground and stamped upon him. The Curate himself then thought that it was enough, and bade them let him alone and go their way.
>
> Some time after Jonathan Maskew came. As soon as he began to speak, the same mob came and pulled him down, and dragged him out of the house. Then they tore off his clothes, and dragged him along upon his naked back over the gravel and pavement. When they thought they had sufficiently bruised him, they let him go, and went away. . . . It was my turn to go next.[2]

He was stoned for two miles along the road after trying to preach, but he recovered from the effects in a fortnight. At Wrangle he was seized by the mob at six in the morning and held captive in a public-house when the parson told them not to let him go:

> So he took me out to the mob, who presently hurried me away, and threw me into a pool of standing water. It took me up to the

---

[1] *Lives*, vol. i, p. 380.　　[2] *Ibid.*, vol. i, p. 71.

neck. Several times I strove to get out, but they pitched me in again. They told me I must go through it seven times. I did so, and then they let me come out. When I had got upon dry ground, a man stood ready with a pot full of white paint. He painted me all over from head to foot, and then they carried me into a public-house again. Here I was kept till they had put five more of our friends into the water. Then they came and took me out again, and carried me to a great pond, which was railed in on every side, being ten or twelve feet deep. Here four men took me by my legs and arms, and swung me backward and forward. For a moment I felt the flesh shrink; but it was quickly gone. I gave myself up to the Lord, and was content His will should be done. . . . They swung me two or three times, and then threw me as far as they could into the water. The fall and the water soon took away my senses, so that I felt nothing more.[1]

He was dragged out and taken to a friend's house, where they put him into bed: but within a few minutes the mob returned and dragged him off again. He refused to promise not to try to preach to them again, but his friend promised for him and again put him into bed. The mob went off and told the parson, who told them to take him out of the parish:

So they came and took me out of bed a second time. But I had no clothes to put on, my own being wet, and also covered with paint. But they put an old coat over me, took me about a mile, and set me upon a little hill. They then shouted three times, 'God save the King and the devil take the Preacher!' . . .
I had much ado to walk or even to stand. I knew not what to do or where to go. . . . One of our friends lived three or four miles off, but I was so weak and ill that it did not seem possible for me to get so far. However, I trusted in God and set out, and at length I got to the house. The family did everything for me that was in their power: they got me clothes, and whatever else was needful. I rested four days with them, in which time my strength was tolerably restored. Then I went into the Circuit, where I met with more persecution. As I was preaching . . .[2]

When he died, an obituary notice referred to his 'slender abilities as a preacher'; but the answer given in *The Minutes of Conference* for 1785 is perhaps fairer to his memory. The usual question is asked, 'Who have died this year?' and the answer

[1] *Lives*, vol. i, p. 75.   [2] *Ibid.*, vol. i, pp. 76–7.

given is, 'Thomas Mitchell, an old soldier of Jesus Christ'.[1]

No brief extracts, however, can do justice to these *Lives of the Early Methodist Preachers*, with their variety of styles and frequent simplicity and vigour of expression. The stories are often moving and dramatic, and Southey's words about John Nelson, one of them, might be applied to nearly all:

John Nelson had as high a spirit, and as brave a heart as ever Englishman was blessed with.

A few critics[2] have recognized the merits of these eighteenth-century autobiographies, but they have been overlooked by the majority of writers, probably because they first appeared in a magazine read by a very limited number of people and chiefly restricted to Methodists. The two collected editions have also been issued by the Methodist Publishing House, which has again tended to cut them off from the literary world. The casual reader hearing of such *Lives* is at first tempted to avoid them, expecting only to find moralizing stories interspersed between long sermons. It is true that all the writers are concerned with religion and with the rise of the Methodist movement, and go into details about their souls, though to an age enthralled by psychology this should be an added attraction. But any serious reader soon finds far more than this as he reads the plain and open stories of

[1] Dr. Caldecott, in *The Religious Sentiment*, remarked on the surprisingly long lives of many of the preachers, and attributes this chiefly to their mental health: 'They worked by night and by day for periods of thirty, forty and even fifty years . . . and after their strenuous labours were concluded by physical decline, many of them lived long evenings of life in gradually diminished service; they all closed in serenity. At the age of seventy-nine, Christopher Hopper writes, "As for the enemy, I know not what has become of him". . . . These were the men who were regarded as "enthusiasts" by the grave moralists who filled most of the ministries of the eighteenth century; but it was an enthusiasm which had the quality of lasting' (p. 30).

[2] For example, the very appreciative tribute to the *Lives* paid by Professor Caldecott in *The Religious Sentiment: An Inductive Enquiry*. F. C. Gill, in *The Romantic Movement and Methodism*, 1937, has an interesting chapter on Coleridge and Methodism, instancing many of his comments and criticisms of the movement. He notes Coleridge's appreciation of these *Lives*. In 1797, Coleridge began a series of letters to his friend, Thomas Poole, in which he proposed to give an account of his own life. He wrote:

'MY DEAR POOLE,—I could inform the dullest author how he might write an interesting book. Let him relate the events of his own life with honesty, not disguising the feelings that accompanied them. I never yet read a Methodist's "Experience" in the *Gospel Magazine* without receiving instruction and amusement.'

men who struggled, worked, and suffered in different parts of Europe and America and among all classes of society, for a cause in which they believed. The adventures of Silas Told, Sampson Staniforth, John Haime, John Nelson, and others are as much like short novels as like religious auto-biographies. At times they seem to show affinities with Smollett and more slightly with Fielding, but I can find no evidence to show that any of the writers ever read their novels. In prose style again, many of them strikingly resemble Defoe. They have the same seeming simplicity and clarity, use the same homely illustrations, and give the same exact details of events in a colloquial manner, but there is no proof that any of them read Defoe. Probably many of them did read novels, because some do mention reading plays and such works as the *Spectator*, but the books they name are always those that might be expected to improve their readers, and other books are simply referred to in general. Bunyan is frequently mentioned and much of their matter is similar, but their style is far more like that of Defoe.

There may be a simple explanation. Wesley invited the preachers to send him accounts of their lives and to write as much as they liked. He promised to omit the unsuitable parts and correct any errors. There is no evidence to show how thoroughly he did this, but ample justification for believing that he would leave out the 'hard words' and simplify any obscure passage. They were also trained and almost drilled in his methods of writing and speaking plainly and without any flourishes and affectation, so that no preacher would be likely to write to him in an ornate or involved style without immediate reproof. Some *Lives* may have been sent to him written in an artificial manner, but these he certainly did not publish. Thus his own great influence encouraged this manner of writing, and his own supervision allowed only those *Lives* to be published which conformed to his standard. This does not imply that there is not difference in style and matter in the various accounts, but it does mean that all fit in with Wesley's standard of 'Perspicuity and purity, propriety, strength and easiness, joined together'.[1]

[1] Wesley to Samuel Furly, *Letters*, vol. iv, p. 256.

OTHER METHODIST WRITERS OF THE
EIGHTEENTH CENTURY

Reasons for few Methodist publications. The *Journal* of Charles Wesley. The works of George Whitefield. Journals and sermons. James Hervey: *Meditations Among the Tombs*; *Dialogues*. John Fletcher of Madeley. Walter Churchey: connection with Cowper and Wesley. Thomas Olivers: Poems. Edward Perronet. Augustus Toplady. John Bakewell. Benjamin Rhodes. John Cennick.

CHAPTER VIII

OTHER METHODIST WRITERS OF THE EIGHTEENTH CENTURY

WHEN a Methodist consulted John Wesley about publishing a book, he replied: 'It is the glory of the Methodists to have *few authors*. And a young man can hardly be too slow in this matter.'[1] He desired his preachers to let him read their works before publication, and not to sing hymns of their own composition. His attitude was probably very wise, and it lessened the amount of Methodist writing during the century. Some Methodists entered into theological and political controversy, some published sermons; but these may now be disregarded. It is sufficient here to review the journals of Charles Wesley and George Whitefield and to give a short account of a few Methodists who have some claims to being poets or hymn writers.[2]

The *Journal* of Charles Wesley is less well known than it deserves, probably owing to the difficulty in securing copies.[3] Thomas Jackson found the manuscripts of it on the floor of a warehouse where the furniture of Charles Wesley, Junior, was stored, and it was not until 1849 that it was first published. It begins in March, 1736, when Charles Wesley arrived at Frederica, a month after going to America, and ends on November 6, 1756. There are many breaks in the record, but it gives vivid pictures of the life in Georgia,

---

[1] *Letters*, vol. vi, p. 324.

[2] I am omitting from this chapter Cowper, Smart, and Blake, for whom claims might be made that they were very strongly influenced by Methodism. They are discussed in chap. x.

[3] In 1909 a small edition was issued by Robert Culley: *The Early Journal of Rev. Charles Wesley*, ed. John Telford. This is now difficult to obtain.

Charles Wesley's conversion, his preaching in prisons, and of the perils from mobs.

John Wesley wrote his *Journal* with the intention of publishing parts of it, but Charles does not seem to have intended to do this, and consequently he is at times more frank in his judgements about people. He seems to have been more able than John to involve himself in furious arguments and religious quarrels, as well as more ready to write about his personal doubts and religious sufferings. Otherwise his *Journal* is extraordinarily like that of his brother in style and matter.

In Georgia he was even less able than John to deal with the lying and hysterical women who spent their time in slandering General Oglethorpe and creating mischief. He was entirely deceived by an adventurer and thief, Mr. Appee, and he was even more stubborn in reviving old practices of the Church of England, such as complete immersion in baptism. Life among the serious and fastidious devotees of religion in Oxford was not a good training for work in a new colony composed of debtors and released prisoners. He has accounts of diabolical cruelty practised on slaves, of 'Mr. Hull whipping a she-slave so long that she fell down at his feet for dead', and of her recovery when dripping hot sealing-wax was put on her flesh, and stories of negroes nailed up by the ears for flogging. He travelled up the American coast in half-rotten boats and with incompetent sailors, bidding farewell to a 'wretched captain who for the last two days had, most happily for us, lain dead drunk on the floor, without sense or motion'. There are pleasant descriptions of the countryside round Boston.

After the return to England, there are accounts of his journeys, visits to great houses and gardens, and dining with nobility. He was always more at home than John with high society, and in his old age held fashionable musical concerts at his house in Marylebone. There are frequent entries referring to his life in higher circles, such as 'I waited on Lady Betty Hastings', and 'I dined with my brother at Lord Oxford's', and 'Lady Oxford, Lord Duplin and the famed Lady Mary were of the company'. John Wesley, had he to mention such company, would probably have observed something about the shallowness of high life, but Charles takes a certain pleasure in writing the names.

He had much less patience with mobs and hysterical converts. Unlike his brother, he met a highwayman:

Tuesday, October 11, 1737. I set out for London. In a mile's riding my horse fell lame. I sang the 91st Psalm, and put myself under the divine protection. I had scarce ended, and turned the hut, on Shotover Hill, when a man came up to me, and demanded my money, showing, but not presenting, a pistol. I gave him my purse. He asked how much there was. 'About thirty shillings.' 'Have you no more?' 'I will see'; put my hand in my pocket and gave him some halfpence. He repeated the question, 'Have you no more?' I had thirty pounds in a private pocket; bade him search himself; which he did not choose. He ordered me to dismount, which I did; but begged hard for my horse again, promising not to pursue him. He took my word, and restored him. I rode gently on, praising God. My bags, and watch, and gold, the robber was *forced* to leave me.[1]

The ways of God were mysterious, but Charles Wesley could find them in any circumstances. His 'conversion' was mixed up with a serious illness in 1738, when at times he seems to have been delirious. He suffered greatly from 'a toothache', and two doctors 'bled me three times, and poured down draughts, oils and apozems without end'. His recovery and the end of his spiritual crisis, his 'conversion', nearly coincided on May 21, 1738.

Possibly the most moving part of his *Journal* is the account of his preaching at Newgate, and of his visits to a 'sick negro in the condemned hole'. As in the stories of Silas Told and Sarah Peters, the absence of sentimental sympathy is remarkable. The preachers went to the criminals, stayed with them till the end, preaching and heartening them, but never doubted the justice of the executions. The twentieth-century man would tend to cry out that such scenes were wrong, but would hesitate about attending the hangings.

In July, 1738, Charles Wesley visited Newgate frequently.

[1] *The Early Journal of the Rev. Charles Wesley*, ed. John Telford, p. 128.

Below is a selection from his description of his work with one 'batch':

July 17. At Newgate I preached on death (which they must suffer the day after to-morrow). . . . The Black was quite happy. The other criminal was in an excellent temper; believing, or on the point of it. . . .

July 19. At six I prayed and sang with them all together. . . . At half-hour past nine their irons were knocked off, and their hands tied. . . . By half-hour past ten we came to Tyburn, waited till eleven; then were brought the children appointed to die. I got upon the cart with Sparks and Broughton. . . . They were all cheerful; full of comfort, peace and triumph; assuredly persuaded Christ had died for them. . . . The Black had spied me coming out of the coach, and saluted me with his looks. As often as his eyes met mine, he smiled with the most composed, delightful countenance I ever saw. . . . None showed any natural terror of death; no fear or crying or tears. I never saw such calm triumph, such incredible indifference to dying. We sang several hymns; particularly,

> 'Behold the Saviour of mankind
> Nailed to the shameful tree'.[1]

. . . I took leave of each in particular. Mr. Broughton bade them not be surprised when the cart should draw away. They cheerfully replied, they should not; expressed some concern how we should get back to our coach. We left them going to meet their Lord, ready for the Bridegroom. When the cart drew off, not one stirred, or struggled for life, but meekly gave up their spirits. Exactly at twelve they were turned off. I spoke a few suitable words to the crowd.[2]

Here, as in most of the *Journal*, when he is not dealing with the state of his soul, we get a clear and restrained account of the life around him. Like John Wesley, he wrote down simply what he saw and described how people behaved in precise terms, though possibly with more dramatic sense. He has no desire to elaborate, and he is not describing events in order to make a reader feel in any particular manner. He does all that is possible for 'those appointed to die', and preaches to the living immediately they 'are turned off'. The feeling of 'sentiment' which was to become so fashionable never touches him. Its place was taken by

---

[1] By his father, Samuel Wesley.
[2] *The Early Journal of Rev. Charles Wesley*, ed. John Telford, p. 189–94.

a sense of duty, imperative on him because he knew he was 'saved'.[1]

. . . . .

Like the Wesleys, George Whitefield published a great number of sermons, different editions of the same sermons, pamphlets, accounts of his life, journals, answers to attacks, and letters. To-day most of these are difficult to obtain because they have seldom been reprinted since the eighteenth century. In 1876 the Rev. L. Tyerman published *The Life of Rev. George Whitefield* in two volumes. This, the best account of his life, contains large extracts from his works, some in their complete form, and is the most convenient source for authorities on anything connected with him. Wherever possible, any quotations from Whitefield's writings in this book are taken from Tyerman's *Life*.

Though Whitefield's works are of great interest to any student of the Methodist revival, often showing rhetorical power and psychological insight, they have not the literary value of the works of the Wesleys, and can be treated here much more briefly. In 1740 he published *A Short Account of God's Dealings with the Rev. Mr. George Whitefield, A.B.*, *Late of Pembroke College, Oxford*, an account of the early years of his life, which was written on board the *Elizabeth* when he sailed to Georgia. He says that he was born in 1714, that his father kept the Bell Inn at Gloucester, and then tells of the sins of his youth quite in the Bunyan manner:

> I can truly say, I was froward from my mother's womb. . . . Lying, filthy talking, and foolish jesting I was much addicted to even when very young. Sometimes I used to curse, if not swear. Stealing from my mother, I thought no theft at all, and used to

---

[1] Only two sermons of Charles Wesley were published in his lifetime. The first was preached by him on April 4, 1742, before the University of Oxford. The text was 'Awake, thou that sleepest' (Ephesians v. 14). It was published the same year and had thirty-six editions at least. The other, 'On the Cause and Cure of Earthquakes', written in 1750, was published in John Wesley's collected sermons. In 1816 his widow published twelve more of his sermons. They have the same type of short sentences as those of John, though they lack his calmer logic and homely metaphors. Contemporary reports stress Charles's power of vivid description and vehement note of personal appeal: 'It was all thunder and lightning.' To me most of this seems lost in the printed sermons.

make no scruple of taking money out of her pocket before she was up. . . . Numbers of Sabbaths have I broken, and generally used to behave myself very irreverently in God's sanctuary. Much money have I spent in plays. . . .

When I was about twelve, I was placed at a school called St. Mary de Crypt, in Gloucester—the last grammar school I ever went to. Having a good elocution and memory, I was remarked for making speeches before the Corporation, at their annual visitation. . . .

During the time of my being at school, I was very fond of reading plays, and have kept from school for days together to prepare myself for acting them.[1]

The account seems harmless enough to-day, though it was considered shocking at the time. Bishop Lavington, in his *Enthusiasm of Methodists and Papists Compared*, blustered at some length, adding finally: 'Mr. Whitefield's account of God's dealings with him is such a boyish, ludicrous, filthy, nasty, and shameless relation of himself, as quite defiles paper, and is shocking to decency and modesty. 'Tis a perfect jakes of uncleanness.'

His youth was spent under more difficult circumstances than that of the Wesleys, and when he went to Pembroke College in 1732 it was as a servitor. All his life, however, he was fond of aristocratic company, and he ever had a tendency to seek out those in important positions. Later on, when he gave accounts of services, he generally managed to mention the names of the distinguished visitors present. A touch of this characteristic is seen in his account of his entry into Oxford:

Soon after my admission to Pembroke College, I found my having been used to a public-house was now of service to me. For many of the servitors being sick at my first coming up, by my diligent and ready attendance I ingratiated myself into the gentlemen's favours so far, that many, who had it in their power, chose me to be their servitor.[2]

When reading his account of his Oxford days, with his sins and his raptures and his readings of Thomas à Kempis, we soon discover the traits in his style that Wesley disliked. He tends to strew his lines with adjectives, particularly with

[1] Tyerman, vol. i, pp. 4–5.   [2] *Ibid.*, vol. i, p. 15.

'dear', 'delightful', 'sweet' and 'blessed'; he loves exclamations and rhetorical repetitions. Wesley called it 'a luscious manner of speaking' and commanded his preachers to avoid it at all costs. It is a style that immediately suggests insincerity, though George Whitefield was no hypocrite. Almost any of his religious writings will illustrate these points, but, for an example, here is an extract describing his work at Oxford:

> Oh, what a delightful life did I lead here! What communion did I daily enjoy with God! How sweetly did my hours in private glide away, in reading and praying over Mr. Henry's Comment upon the Scriptures! Nor was I alone happy: for several dear youths were quickened greatly, and met daily at my room to build up each other in their most holy faith.[1]

As a young man he was more of a realist than the Wesleys, and less devoted to legalism and rigid observance of rules better forgotten. He soon began to take collections for schools and orphanages at his services, and it remained characteristic of him throughout his life, when describing any service, to state the amount of the collection as well as his distinguished visitors. Thus he made plans and took collections for an orphanage in Georgia, and when he set out on his missionary work there he carried with him quantities of useful materials. The list of the goods that he took with him makes interesting reading and is reminiscent of Robinson Crusoe's rescues from the wreck. His fame as a preacher was already assured before he set out, and the *Gentleman's Magazine* for November, 1737, printed a poem in honour of his sailing. It began:

> How great, how just thy zeal, advent'rous youth!
> To spread, in heathen climes, the light of truth!
> Go, loved of heaven! with every grace refined,
> Inform, enrapture each dark Indian's mind. . . .

When John Wesley left for Georgia in 1735, he took with him 550 copies of a treatise on the Lord's Supper and many other devotional books, but Whitefield's cargo was far more extensive. He bought several hundred pounds' worth of

---

[1] Tyerman, vol. i, p. 57.

assorted goods, which, in addition to books, consisted of such things as six dozen women's caps, twenty-four striped flannel waistcoats, twelve dozens of shirt buttons, a dozen tin pots, sixteen dozens of corks, two dozen leather ink-pots, 100 lemons from Gibraltar, thirteen penknives for Savannah School, many drugs and tools, cloves, onions, and sage, and two hogsheads of fine white wine.

George Whitefield was a great success in Georgia. He disagreed with the policy of Oglethorpe and the Wesleys, who opposed any slavery in the colony, and he gave his support to those who advocated the introduction of slave labour. He wrote: 'The people were denied the use of both rum and slaves. . . . The scheme was well meant at home, but was absolutely impracticable in so hot a country abroad.'[1] He felt himself to be a man of the world, and had few doubts about his own ability and perfect judgement. His character is well seen in many extracts from his journal,[2] though the more youthful parts often suggest his less pleasing characteristics. He always notices his own success, the important people who heard him, and is not above remarking on a good dinner. For example, at Gibraltar in 1738:

March 5. Went to the church belonging to the garrison; preached to a most thronged audience. . . . Both the generals were there, and near fifty communicants. The weekly collection for the poor was larger than was ever known; and —— was so affected, that he wished himself a despised Methodist. Dined at Governor Sabine's, and, at the request of the inhabitants and gentlemen of the garrison, preached again in the afternoon.[3]

These extracts possibly tend to give a more unfavourable picture of Whitefield than he deserves and do not suggest the vitality and power that drew all classes of society to hear him. His writings, however, lack the charm, the ironic humour, the serenity and balance of those of John Wesley; they tend to express unctuous and seemingly over-pious sentiments;

[1] Tyerman, vol. i, p. 141.

[2] Whitefield sent some of his early journals to Charles Wesley for correction. Wesley's note in his own *Journal* is characteristic: '*August 3, 1738.* I corrected Mr. Whitefield's Journal for the Press; my advice to suppress it being over-ruled.'

[3] Tyerman, vol. i, p. 119.

and they lack Wesley's constant use of quotation and his frequent references to literature.

Whitefield's fame was built up on his powers of dramatic oratory, and huge crowds, consisting of all classes of people, flocked to listen to him. Both he and the Wesleys probably overestimated their crowds at times—for it seems unlikely that 80,000 people, as they state sometimes, could possibly have heard them speak. It is difficult to form any idea to-day of his effect on these huge crowds, because passionate, rhetorical oratory reads so coldly, and Whitefield's voice and gestures and power of adapting his matter to his particular audience cannot be recaptured. Of his 18,000 sermons, sixty-three authentic discourses remain, and for an example of his methods here is an extract from that on 'Peter's Denial of his Lord'. He describes Peter repenting:

Methinks I see him wringing his hands, rending his garments, stamping on the ground, and, with the self-condemned publican, smiting upon his breast. See how it heaves! O what piteous sighs and groans are those which come from the very bottom of his heart. Alas! it is too big to speak; but his tears, his briny, bitter, repenting tears, plainly bespeak this to be the language of his awakened soul. 'Alas! where have I been? On the devil's ground. With whom have I been conversing? The devil's children. What is this that I have done? Denied the Lord of Glory; with oaths and curses, denied that I ever knew Him. And now whither shall I go? Or where shall I hide my guilty head? I have sinned against light. I have sinned against repeated tokens of His dear, distinguishing, and heavenly love. I have sinned against repeated warnings, resolutions, promises, and vows. I have sinned openly in the face of the sun, and in the presence of my Master's enemies; and, thereby, have caused His name to be blasphemed. How can I think of being suffered to behold the face of, much less to be employed by, the ever-blessed Jesus any more? O Peter! thou hast undone thyself. Justly mayest thou be thrown aside like a broken vessel. God be merciful to me a sinner.'[1]

One can imagine something of the effect that a great actor could obtain with passages like this, especially when he had a large and sympathetic crowd before him. At times, too, he was the master of a telling and epigrammatic phrase, and could combine this with a quick topical reference. But Whitefield's power was oral, and his writings now live chiefly

[1] Tyerman, vol. ii, p. 297.

as illustrations of this rather than as literature of merit in itself.

. . . . .

Probably the most famous Methodist writer, outside the Wesley family, was James Hervey, who was one of the original members of the Holy Club at Oxford and a close friend of Wesley for many years afterwards. His health was always poor, and this seems to have encouraged the morbid side of his gentle nature. Leaving Oxford, he retired to the peace of Weston-Favel and became increasingly Calvinistic, though for many years he corresponded with Wesley. It was to him that Wesley wrote, explaining his work: 'I look upon all the world as my parish; thus far I mean, that in whatever part of it I am I judge it meet, right, and my bounden duty to declare unto all that are willing to hear, the glad tidings of salvation.'[1]

He was greatly shocked when Wesley began field preaching, and still more astonished when it was suggested that he might join him: 'I a thundering Boanerges! I a trumpet speaking from Heaven! I lift up my voice to the whole world and make the canopy of the skies sing! Never, dear sir.' He went on to invite 'my dear Mr. Wesley' to settle quietly in a parish. Their friendship continued and it was not till the closing years of his life, when he seems to have been very ill, that he published letters between himself and Wesley on the subject of Calvinism. In 1755 he published his views under the title of *Theron and Aspasia*, but the bitterness of his later letters needs the excuse of illness to explain them.

He owed his fame to his *Meditations among the Tombs*, published in 1745,[2] and which achieved enormous popularity during the century, having in all twenty-five editions. He was a keen classical scholar, an admirer of Milton, and wished to retouch and reprint the poems of Giles and Phineas Fletcher.[3] Young's *Night Thoughts* and Thomson's

[1] *Letters*, vol. i, p. 286.
[2] See (a) *Cambridge History of English Literature*, vol. x, chap. xv; (b) *A Survey of English Literature, 1730–1780*, by Oliver Elton, vol. ii, p. 229.
[3] Elton, *op. cit.*, vol. ii, p. 229.

Seasons influenced him, and he entered fully into the spirit of the Churchyard writers.[1] He had a taste for the morbidly sentimental that left most of them looking healthy. He had also a most florid style, a 'kind of tumid and over-ornamented rhetoric which has an extraordinary attraction to half-educated minds',[2] but he was possessed with a love of Nature which makes him important when considering the revival of Romanticism. He followed up *Meditations among the Tombs* with *Reflections on a Flower Garden, Contemplations on the Night,* and *Contemplations on the Starry Heavens.*[3]

Amidst the gruesome revellings in the graveyards—and no man, surely, so smacked his lips in appreciation of the 'riots of the reptiles' there—he often introduces exceedingly accurate touches of Nature observation. He has Thomson's love of listing flowers by name and adding careful descriptions, and seems to have a genuine liking for the country, when he can cease to gloat over the maudlin elements around him. Possibly eighteenth-century gentlemen found pleasure in reading his prose aloud in solemn tones. When Hervey begins to brood, he writes:

Examining the records of mortality, I found the memorials of a promiscuous multitude. . . . The once gay and gallant Fidelio sleeps in other embraces, even in the icy arms of death. . . . Poor Chremylus . . . arose from the diversions of a card-table and dropt into the dwellings of darkness. One night Corinna was all gaiety . . . the next night she lay stiff and pale, an extended corpse, and ready to be mingled with the moldering dead. . . . Instead of sumptuous tables, and delicious treats, the poor voluptuary is himself a feast for fattened insects; the reptile riots in his flesh.

It must have been a joy to read aloud this sounding prose with its constant alliteration, especially if the reader was

---

[1] See 'Ode to Fancy', by Joseph Warton:
> Let us with silent footsteps go
> To charnels and the house of woe,
> To Gothic churches, vaults, and tombs,
> Where each sad night some virgin comes
> With throbbing breast, and faded cheek,
> Her promis'd bridegroom's urn to seek. . . .

[2] *A History of England in the Eighteenth Century*, by W. E. H. Lecky, vol. iii.

[3] *Meditations and Contemplations* (in two volumes), by James Hervey, A.B., 1748. This contains all the four parts.

trying to impress a frivolous family. Hervey loves the poetic diction of his age, and he is happy when 'feathered songsters in the circumambient air pass over the fluid scenery', though he can turn sometimes to more direct description:

Not long ago, I happened to spy a thoughtless jay. The poor bird was idly busied in dressing his pretty plumes or hopping carelessly from spray to spray. A sportsman, coming by, observes the feathered rover. Immediately he lifts the tube, and levels his blow. Swifter than the whirlwind flies the leaden death; and in a moment, lays the silly creature breathless on the ground.—Such, such, may be the fate of the man, who . . .

He can describe accurately when he chooses, and we are sometimes surprised with vivid phrases: 'The river . . . spreads itself far and wide, and buries the meadow under a brown, sluggish, soaking deluge.' 'The grass is intermingled with moss and embroidered with flowers.' 'Yonder struts a pretty fellow that seems to have dipped his plumes in the rainbow.'

Dialogue 8 of the *Dialogues between Theron and Aspasio* is on the wickedness of duelling and is of interest because it has so many phrases like those used in Sheridan's *The Rivals*.[1] There are, for example: 'A heinous offence', 'But Honour, my Aspasio, Honour is at stake', 'Better lose our life than forfeit our reputation', 'To indite a formal challenge'. These and several other phrases are repeated in the scene between Bob Acres and David in Sheridan's play. Possibly Sheridan was deliberately alluding to Hervey's book, which was then well known.

It was not the kind of prose that John Wesley liked, and in writing a reply to Hervey he said, 'Is not the descriptions often too laboured, and the language too stiff and affected?' It may be said that Hervey's language is inspired chiefly by bad taste, and that he exhibits the most morbid sentiments of the age; but he also shows the influence of the Evangelical movement on the literature of the time. In him can be seen the 'sentimentalism' then so popular, the passion for moralization, and something more than a common love

[1] *The Rivals* was first produced in 1775.

for Nature. This Evangelical spirit was having its effect outside the Methodist movement, and several of the 'graveyard' writers favoured their doctrines. Robert Blair, the author of *The Grave*, was 'an evangelical, a practical and a powerful preacher',[1] and Wesley thought highly of Edward Young. Hervey joined this class of writers easily and excelled in his task 'to paint the gloomy horrors of the tomb'.[2] He illustrates the background of serious middle-class life of the period, and preaches with sentiment, but he never enters into the dynamic spirit of Methodism, with its songs and emotional certainty of salvation. Just as he shows slight signs of the returning love of Nature and revival of Romanticism,[3] so he shows the outside only of the Evangelical doctrines. To-day he seems to illustrate chiefly their unpleasant characteristics, their emotion, their morbidity and their moralization. The Methodist preachers had to advance beyond this before they were to affect English life.

·   ·   ·   ·   ·

A short reference must be made to the Rev. John Fletcher, the most charming of all Wesley's followers. A Swiss by birth, he became a soldier of fortune and served in Portugal and Brazil before settling in England as a tutor. Later he entered the Church and became a close friend of Wesley. After acting as Superintendent of Lady Huntingdon's college at Trevecca, he parted from it owing to his Arminian views, and became Vicar of Madeley in Shropshire. Wesley thought so highly of him that once, when he was ill, he nominated Fletcher as his successor in leadership of the movement. When Fletcher died, Wesley preached his funeral sermon from the text, 'Mark the perfect man, and behold the upright, for the end of that man is peace'.

Fletcher has caught the hearts of all who have studied him. Of him Southey said:

No age or country has ever produced a man of more fervent piety, or more perfect charity; no church has ever possessed a more

[1] *Poetical Works of Robert Blair*, Life by Rev. G. Gilfillan, 1854.
[2] *The Grave* (Blair), line 5.
[3] See chap. xi for further discussion of Romanticism.

apostolic minister. . . . If ever true Christian charity was manifested in polemical writing, it was by Fletcher of Madeley. Even theological controversy never in the slightest degree irritated his heavenly temper.[1]

Another critic has said:

He was the St. Francis of early Methodism and it seems the most natural thing in the world to be told that, one day, he took a robin for his text. If other leaders of the movement were stern, his was always the voice of tenderness and charity.[2]

His writings were all controversial and were chiefly concerned with defending Wesley's position in regard to the American war and the Calvinists. The most important in their time were the *Checks to Antinomianism*, which appeared in the form of five series of letters between 1771 and 1773.

Though at times he has a slight tendency to gloom like James Hervey, his argument is placid and conciliatory, and his points are illustrated with homely illustrations and gentle irony and wit. It is a pity that his writings were confined to theological problems which are of little interest to-day, because the charm and saintliness which lies behind all his controversial pamphlets might have produced a real work of art. As an example of his power of vivid illustration, here is an extract from the second *Check*, where he is meeting the charge that the Arminians thought they were saved by their own merits. He pictures a village scene:

'Thomas, I stand here before the judge, accused of having robbed the Rev. Mr. Shirley, near Bath, last month on such an evening. Can you speak a word for me?' Thomas turns to the judge and says, 'Please, your honour, the accusation is false, for our parson was in Madeley-Wood, and I can make an oath of it, for he even reproved me for swearing at our pit's mouth that very evening'. By his evidence the judge acquits me. 'Now, sir, ask cursing Tom whether I am acquitted and *justified* by his *merits*, or by the simple evidence? Though I am no scholar, I know very well that if our Methodist parson is not hanged, it is none of my deservings.' Thus, Sir, an ignorant collier, as great a stranger to your metaphysics as you are

---

[1] *Life of John Wesley*, by Robert Southey, chap. xxv.
[2] W. H. Hutton in *Cambridge History of English Literature*, x, p. 367.

to his mandrell, discovers at once a material difference between justification by the *evidence* and justification by the *merits* of a witness.[1]

• • • • •

A very minor writer, but one of some interest, was Walter Churchey, a frequent correspondent of Wesley and a friend of Cowper. He was a Welsh lawyer and lived at Hay, Brecon, where he had a large family and very little business. As well as being a keen Methodist, he read poetry and had some claims to being a critic. John Wesley consulted him about the *Arminian Magazine* and the publication of some of Charles Wesley's poems, though he never seems to have followed any of his advice. In this he was probably quite right. Churchey was also a writer of verse with an ambition to see it published, though a biographer has said that 'it is not generally accepted as poetry'.

Churchey's chief interest to us lies in the fact that both Wesley and Cowper wrote to him about publishing a vast quarto of his poetical works. He sent both of them a great parcel of his manuscripts and asked for comments, laying stress on his most learned attempt, a verse translation of *The Art of Painting* from the Latin of Alphonse du Fresnoy. Wesley wrote back and said he found many very good lines but nothing which moved the passions or was 'sentimental'.

Therefore no bookseller would venture to buy them, as knowing they will not sell. And they lay utterly out of the way of the Methodists, who do not care to buy or even read (at least the generality of them) any but religious books. I do not believe all my influence would induce them to buy as many copies as would suffice to pay for the printing.[2]

This seems to have discouraged Churchey; for Wesley writes a few weeks later: 'I think it is a pity to burn the poems.'[3] William Cowper wrote to him on December 13, 1786, and said:

I congratulate you on your possession of a poetical talent, which at such hours of leisure you can win from a profession the least

---

[1] Fletcher's works have not been reprinted since the early nineteenth century, but an account of them, with extracts, is given in *Arminianism*, by A. W. Harrison, 1937.

[2] *Letters*, vol. viii, p. 82.   [3] *Ibid.*, vol. viii, p. 94.

amusing in the world, must afford you often an agreeable enter-tainment. I find your versification smooth, your language correct and forcible. . . . But you ask me, would I advise you to publish? I would advise every man to publish whose subjects are well chosen, whose sentiments are just, and who can afford to be a loser. . . . For my own part I could no more amuse myself with writing verse, if I did not print it when written, than with the study of tactics.[1]

He told Churchey that it was a pleasant recreation for him, but that publication would be expensive. The end of the letter was concerned with the cheapest method of getting the load of manuscripts back to Brecon. Churchey continued to write to Wesley about publication, and at last set about finding subscribers, while Wesley warned him that many who promised him would not pay up: 'We must not imagine that *all* who promise will perform.' To help Churchey, he had printed at his own press, the following pamphlet, which he distributed himself to likely Methodist subscribers:[2]

PROPOSALS

For printing by subscription *Poems on Various Occasions*
By Walter Churchey, Gent.

Conditions.

1. The work will be compressed in one large quarto volume.
2. It will be printed on a fine paper and with a good type.
3. The price is one guinea. . . .
5. The book will be delivered about the 1st of July next.

Mr. Churchey is an honest attorney! Therefore he is poor, and has eight children. Give me a guinea for him, for his own sake, for God's sake, and for the sake of

JOHN WESLEY.

BRISTOL.
March 3, 1789.

Letters follow from Wesley to Churchey, containing phrases like the following:

It was a deadly step not to secure half the money at the time of subscription. I receive the whole. . . . As you are not a stripling I wonder you have not yet learned the difference between *promise* and *performance*.[3]

However, the big quarto of 858 pages was entered at

---

[1] *The Life and Works of William Cowper*, by Robert Southey, 1837, vol. xv, pp. 188–9.

[2] *Letters*, vol. viii, p. 121.   [3] *Ibid.*, vol. viii, pp. 134, 138.

Stationer's Hall in 1789. Wesley sent him 100 guineas which he had collected and said he hoped to send fifty more. The list of subscribers in the front of the book contains the names of many Methodist preachers and some Oxford dons. The contents include:

The Art of Painting, Imitations of Spenser, Shakespeare, Milton, Butler, Young, Thomson, Gay, Pope, Swift and Churchill. Lines on Mr. Dodd. *Joseph*, or the Viceroy of Egypt, a poem of twelve books with notes.

There are also some shorter poems besides these long, dull works. Parts of his poem 'On a Mare' might be verse written for children:

> Jet gentle jogs four miles an hour,
> Trots safe, if stinted to the four,
> Enjoys the tramels of a cart
> And eats good grass with all her heart. . . .
>   Her back, not over round or flat,
>   Is bare of skin as well as fat.

Cowper wrote again to Churchey on December 24, 1790, thanking him for remarks on his edition of Homer, and then commenting on reviews of Churchey's *Poems*:

To say that I was grieved at the treatment you have received from the Reviewers is saying little, for I felt myself not more grieved than angry. To censure a book in that general manner is neither just to the author of it, nor satisfactory to their own readers. Extracts should always be given. . . .

I never feel myself poor but when I see or hear of a valuable man whose exigencies exceed my ability to relieve them. How heartily and gladly I would administer to the complete removal of yours were it in my power, God knows.[1]

Anyone who tries to read much of Churchey's poetry to-day will tend to sympathize with the eighteenth-century reviewers, though Churchey is often competent enough, and has a good knowledge of English poetry. His chief interest now lies in the letters written to him by Cowper and Wesley, and in the attempts he seems to have made to arrange a meeting between these two men.[2]

· · · · ·

[1] *The Works of William Cowper*, ed. R. Southey, 1837, vol. xv, p. 225.
[2] See chap. vi.

An account of the life of Thomas Olivers was given in the chapter on 'Methodist Autobiography', but a little more ought to be said of this man who was of some importance in his own time. Well educated and with the ability to write clear prose, he wrote numerous letters and pamphlets about Calvinism against those of Toplady and Rowland Hill. Wesley saw his ability and soon made him the Editor of the *Arminian Magazine*. But in 1789 he wrote in his *Journal*:

> I settled all my temporal business, and, in particular, chose a new person to prepare the *Arminian Magazine*, being obliged, however unwillingly, to drop Mr. O——, for only these two reasons:
> 1. The errata are unsufferable. I have borne them for these twelve years, but can bear them no longer.
> 2. Several pieces are inserted without my knowledge, both in prose and verse. I must try whether these things cannot be amended for the short residue of my life.[1]

Olivers was fond of music and wrote a tune that is still sung in churches, *Helmsley* ('Lo! He comes with clouds descending'). In 1770 he heard a famous Jewish singer, Leoni, who gave him a melody. With this in his mind he returned and wrote a religious poem from which the well-known hymn, 'The God of Abraham praise', is taken. Many critics have highly praised this for its power and beauty, claiming that 'it will be sung with delight and profit as long as the English language is understood'.[2] The first verse is:

> The God of Abraham praise,
>   Who reigns enthroned above,
> Ancient of everlasting days,
>   And God of love.
> Jehovah! Great I AM!
>   By earth and heaven confessed;
> I bow and bless the sacred name
>   For ever blessed.

He published several short pamphlets of religious verse, and in 1791 wrote *A Descriptive and Plaintive Elegy on the Death of the late Rev. John Wesley*. This was published in a pamphlet of

[1] *Journal*, vol. vii, p. 525.

[2] An account of Thomas Olivers, with the opinions of various critics of his hymn, is given in *The Methodist Hymn-Book Illustrated*, by John Telford, 1906, pp. 241–4.

twenty-four pages, and consisted of eighty-two stanzas. Most of it is in a kind of pastoral vein, with swains and shepherds mourning for the death of Wesley:

> As on the hills the watchful shepherd stands
> He hears the tale below and lifts his hands;
> Then sighs, and smites his breast, and drowns his path with tears,
> And to his lonely cot the mournful tidings bears!

After the Passions, Storms, and Zephyrs have mourned for him an account of his life is given:

> He often rode, as through the land he past,
> Full thirty miles, before he broke his fast!
> Then added thirty more, before he stopped to dine!
> And ten or twenty more, before his preaching time!

> To live for God, while in this vale of Tears,
> He rose at four o'clock, for three score years! . . .
> Nor did he ever cease, while we had time to hear;
> But preach'd, or sometimes taught, *a thousand times a year*!

Like Thomas Olivers, a few other Methodists wrote some bad verse and a few great hymns during the century. Edward Perronet, the son of Vincent Perronet, Vicar of Shoreham, and the friend of Wesley, wrote a satire[1] on the Church of England which he called *The Mitre*. When John Wesley read it, he considered that it was an attack on the Church and persuaded Perronet to withdraw it. He is remembered to-day as the author of:

> All hail the power of Jesu's name;
> Let angels prostrate fall;
> Bring forth the royal diadem
> To crown Him Lord of all.

A few other Methodist writers of hymns ought to have a brief mention.

Augustus Montague Toplady, 1740–78, was converted by the Methodists and became Vicar of Broadhembury,

---

[1] The British Museum has a copy with some notes in the author's hand-writing. Its title is *The Mitre, A Sacred Poem*, by Edward Perronet, 1757 ('suppressed by private authority'). It has 279 pages of very tedious satire on the bishops and their love of dress and power. The footnotes suggest that as all clergymen behave with the seriousness of their Methodist brethren the Church of England will improve. Wesley's advice to his followers seems to have been very wise regarding publication.

before he came to London to preach and to edit the *Gospel Magazine*, which stated the case for the Calvinistic section of the Evangelical revival. In this magazine, in 1776, he wrote an article at the end of which was the famous hymn, 'Rock of Ages, cleft for me'. Of this Dr. Julian, in *The Dictionary of Hymnology*, has said: 'No other English hymn can be named which has laid so broad and firm a grasp upon the English-speaking world.' In 1776 he published a book, *Psalms and Hymns*, but most of his other works are now forgotten.

John Bakewell, 1721–1819, conducted the Greenwich Park Academy, and became one of Wesley's preachers in 1749. His hymn, 'Hail, Thou once despised Jesus', first appeared in 1757. The present first line, however, was written by Toplady when he included the hymn in his *Psalms and Hymns*. The original line, which seemed directed against Calvinistic beliefs, was 'Hail, Thou universal Saviour'. The hymn seems to catch that lyrical quality and that note of rapture which either drew men into the Methodist movement or strongly repelled them:

> Worship, honour, power, and blessing,
> Thou art worthy to receive;
> Loudest praises without ceasing,
> Meet it is for us to give.
> Help, ye bright, angelic spirits!
> Bring your sweetest noblest lays;
> Help to sing our Saviour's merits,
> Help to chant Immanuel's praise!

Benjamin Rhodes, 1743–1815, was the son of a schoolmaster and had a good education. He became one of Wesley's preachers in 1766 and was famous for his fine singing voice. In 1787 he wrote a poem in four parts, which he entitled *Messiah*. The first part of this is the well-known hymn, the first verse of which is:

> My heart and voice I raise,
> To spread Messiah's praise;
> Messiah's praise let all repeat;
> The universal Lord,
> By whose almighty word
> Creation rose in form complete.

John Cennick, 1718–55, was for a time a teacher at Wesley's school, Kingswood, before he joined Whitefield. Finally, he became a Moravian, and was a successful preacher both in Ireland and in Germany. Charles Wesley revised some of his early hymns, of which three are frequently sung to-day. These were first published in 1742, in *Sacred Hymns for the Children of God in the Days of Their Pilgrimage*. Their chief characteristic is that of joy and rapture. The first one begins:

> Thou great Redeemer, dying Lamb,
>   We love to hear of Thee;
> No music's like Thy charming name,
>   Nor half so sweet can be.

The second has the same emphasis on song:

> Children of the heavenly King,
>   As ye journey sweetly sing;
> Sing your Saviour's worthy praise,
>   Glorious in His works and ways.

The last is an evening hymn, beginning:

> Ere I sleep, for every favour
>   This day showed
>   By my God,
> I will bless my Saviour.[1]

Except for the sermons and controversial pamphlets and articles, these were the chief Methodist writers in the eighteenth century. Their output was small and, except for James Hervey, had little direct influence on the literature of the time. The writings of John Wesley far outweigh all the rest of the Methodist publications together. This does not mean that there was no merit in any other Methodist writings; for a case for the literary value of the *Lives of the Early Preachers*, and for the depth and beauty of many of Charles Wesley's poems has already been made out. The journals of Charles Wesley and of George Whitefield contain

[1] Accounts of these hymn writers are to be found in: *The Dictionary of Hymnology*, ed. Dr. Julian, and *The Methodist Hymn-Book Illustrated*, by John Telford. There are also references in Wesley's *Journal* and *Letters* and in *The Lives of the Early Methodist Preachers*.

many vivid accounts of eighteenth-century life, and will probably be read more widely in the future. James Hervey's *Meditations*, which were popular and important in their own time, are still of value to those studying the rise of Romanticism, and contain many passages of sombre beauty. Many of the hymns written by other Methodists have been sung by thousands of people of different classes and sects ever since they were written. Nevertheless, the direct contribution of Methodism to literature was small in comparison with its effect on all classes of society. Its importance lies far more in the reactions of literary men towards it, and in its effect on English thought and life.

METHODISTS AND THE THEATRE IN THE EIGHTEENTH CENTURY

The theatre of the age. John Wesley and plays. The actors and Methodism. Attacks on Whitefield. *The Minor*. *The Register Office*. *The Methodist*. *The Hypocrite*. Mrs. Bellamy and Tate Wilkinson. Methodist dislike of theatres increases.

Chapter IX

METHODISTS AND THE THEATRE IN THE EIGHTEENTH CENTURY

'When you see the players on the stage, you see the Devil's children grinning at you', said George Whitefield in a sermon. This is often taken as the typical Methodist attitude towards all drama, but it is necessary to look further and deeper before settling the matter so easily in a sentence. Most respectable middle-class citizens would have agreed with Whitefield's view, although they distrusted his religious opinions, because in London and the big towns the theatre was not only supposed to encourage immorality and loose living by its teaching on the stage, but often formed a centre for houses used for brothels and gin-drinking.[1] The bad characters of a city tended to congregate around the play-house. Thus, when a manager tried to open a theatre in a town, he frequently met with fierce opposition from the mayor and town officials as well as from merchants and employers. For example, at Nottingham and Bristol, the introduction of a theatre was opposed on the ground that it would encourage indolence, debauchery, and idleness among young men who ought to be at work.

The first half of the century, however, saw the rise of several great London theatres[2] as well as the beginning of regular performances in some other large towns, and theatres like Drury Lane and the Haymarket attracted a more sober and intelligent audience when great actors such as Garrick played. Even then, however, it caused great

[1] See *London in the Eighteenth Century*, by M. D. George. Numerous letters, petitions and newspaper articles supporting this view are quoted here, pp. 286–9.
[2] See *A History of Early Eighteenth-Century Drama, 1700–1750*, by Allardyce Nicoll, 1925.

scandal when a clergyman like Charles Churchill frequently attended. Except for the great London companies, other actors were suspected as vagabonds of low morality, and strolling bands of players had always to secure the permission of the mayor of a town before they dared to play. Such companies often appeared at fairs and played in booths or barns when given permission, and they are well described by Charles Churchill in his poem *The Apology*:

> The strolling tribe, a despicable race!
> Like wandering Arabs, shift from place to place.
> Vagrants by law, to justice open laid,
> They tremble, of the beadle's lash afraid;
> And, fawning, cringe for wretched means of life
> To Madam Mayoress, or his Worship's wife.[1]

Hogarth has a celebrated print of such a group entitled 'Strolling Actresses dancing in a Barn'. Lower-class people might attend these performances and the more dashing of the aristocracy might look in, but on the whole the more sober members of the middle class and upper class kept away and regarded them with suspicion and dislike.[2]

In his younger days, John Wesley was deeply interested in the theatre, and when in London went to watch performances. In 1729 he saw *The Scornful Lady*[3] at the old Playhouse, and possibly about this time saw *Macbeth* at Drury Lane. This made a deep impression on him, for when in 1750 he met a certain Mr. Griffith, he called him a 'clumsy, overgrown, hard-faced man, whose countenance I could only compare to that (which I saw in Drury Lane thirty years ago) of one of the ruffians in *Macbeth*'.[4] He probably saw other plays, but he certainly read many, for his diary contains numerous references to *The Alchemist*, Otway's *The Orphan*, Rowe's *Royal Convert* and *Jane Shore*, Charles Molloy's

---

[1] *The Apology*, ll. 206–11.

[2] Of course, there were theatres at some of the larger and more aristocratic towns in the country, and these increased in number towards the middle and second half of the century. See the accounts of Foote, Tate Wilkinson, Mrs. Bellamy, and Garrick.

[3] *The Scornful Lady*, by Beaumont and Fletcher, was acted at Drury Lane on February 24, 1729 (Genest, vol. iii, p. 255).

[4] *Journal*, vol. iii, p. 460.

Half-Pay Officers, and many Shakespeare plays. But as he fell under the influence of William Law, his views became stricter and he began to seek salvation by works and abstention from pleasures. Law stated that 'the playhouse is as certainly the house of the devil as the Church is the house of God'.[1] Thus he confined his interest in drama to reading the pocket copy of Shakespeare which he carried with him. After Wesley's death, John Pawson, who lived in his house in City Road in 1797, discovered the annotated copy of Shakespeare and carefully destroyed it.

Wesley held, however, the usual serious-minded view of the time, and took a kind of ironic pleasure in preaching in rooms used for theatres in Birmingham and Wigan, and when a terrible thunderstorm interrupted his sermon at Wapping, he noted in his journal that it frightened the actors at Drury Lane who were playing *Macbeth* with 'mock thunder'. In 1764 he heard that permission was being asked to erect a playhouse in Bristol, so, after consulting Charles, he wrote to the authorities there, thanked them for past civility and added:

> The endeavours lately used to procure subscriptions for building a new playhouse in Bristol have given us not a little concern; and that on various accounts: not barely as most of the present stage entertainments sap the foundation of all religion . . . but as they are peculiarly hurtful to a trading city, giving a wrong turn to youth especially . . . and as drinking and debauchery of every kind are constant attendants on these entertainments, with indolence, effeminacy, and idleness, which affect trade in an high degree.[2]

He then reminded them that Nottingham had just refused permission for a theatre to be opened there for similar reasons. The controversy between Methodists and the theatre managers was just at its height then, as will be shown later, and this possibly influenced his letter. Wesley himself was never opposed to dramatic entertainments for their own sake, though he sometimes opposed them as encouraging idleness and vice. In 1768 he went to see the Westminster

[1] See *The Absolute Unlawfulness of the Stage Entertainment fully Demonstrated*, by W. Law, 1726. There are also references in his other works.
[2] *Letters*, vol. iv, p. 279.

scholars act their annual play, and in December wrote in his journal:

> I saw the Westminster Scholars act the *Adelphi* of Terence, an entertainment not unworthy of a Christian. Oh, how do these heathens shame us! Their very comedies contain both excellent sense, the liveliest pictures of men and manners, and so fine strokes of genuine morality as are seldom found in the writings of Christians.[1]

In 1755, John Home, a minister of the Kirk of Scotland, had a play, *Douglas*, acted in Edinburgh. This aroused fierce controversy and finally Home resigned from the Church. Wesley read the play two years later, and wrote in his journal:

> To-day *Douglas*, the play which has made so much noise, was put into my hands. I was astonished to find it is one of the finest tragedies I ever read. What pity that a few lines were not left out and that it was ever acted at Edinburgh.[2]

This seems to suggest that he thought it might have been acted with success elsewhere, and no one would have been offended. The play was, however, acted in London, so Wesley may have implied that it was better read. Enough has probably been said to show that Wesley himself had no fierce feelings against the drama and theatres, though he disapproved of much that was connected with them.

Charles Wesley had similar views, though, as Captain of Westminster School in 1725, he took the part of Davus, and spoke the Prologue to Terence's *Andria*, which was performed that year. In later years he was more concerned with music, and his house in Marylebone became the centre of a fashionable concert world, when foreign ambassadors, bishops, and many of the nobility came to hear his children play, and John Wesley called in with his wife to demonstrate to his supporters that there was no sin in such entertainments.

But it was not the Wesleys but George Whitefield who attracted most public attention before 1770 and who was most concerned with the theatre.[3] At Gloucester, as a boy,

---

[1] *Journal*, vol. v, p. 294.
[2] *Ibid.*, vol. iv, p. 218.
[3] The best and fullest account of Whitefield is found in *The Life of George Whitefield*, by Luke Tyerman, 1876. A more recent and biased account is in *George Whitefield—The Awakener*, by A. D. Belden, 1931.

he had loved acting and is said to have played truant to learn his various parts. He was only twenty-two when he first came to London and drew crowds to hear his dramatic preaching. He was always an actor who understood exactly how to hold and influence his audience, though there is no reason to doubt his sincerity at the same time. David Garrick often went to hear him preach, and once said he would give £100 if he 'could only say "Oh!" like Mr. Whitefield', and Horace Walpole described him as having all 'the fascinations of a Garrick'. His powers are illustrated in the well-known story of how Lord Chesterfield went to hear him preach. Whitefield described a blind man dropping his stick near the edge of a precipice and groping forward to pick it up again. So intense was the interest as the blind man reached the extreme edge that Chesterfield leaped from his chair and shouted, 'By God! He's over!' Benjamin Franklin describes how men left all money at home before hearing Whitefield preach because they knew he would draw every penny from their pockets for his Orphan House in Georgia.

Tate Wilkinson, a famous actor of the time, greatly disliked the Methodists and afterwards attacked them in his memoirs.[1] He says that 'Whitefield had been really and truly an actor on the stage in his youth', but had left it because 'his squint caused ladies to laugh instead of cry when he played in tragedy'. Another famous comic actor, Edward Shuter, became a follower of Whitefield. Tate Wilkinson says of him that he made large gifts to the Tabernacle, became 'one of the new-born', and wished to go a-preaching because he believed he had a call. These feelings came most strongly on him when he was drunk. So great was Whitefield's liking for Shuter, asserts Wilkinson, that when he had a benefit performance, Whitefield told the congregation at the Tabernacle that they might attend that single show without sinning. It would be foolish to believe much that Tate Wilkinson wrote, but Shuter certainly followed Whitefield, and there are some other references which seem to apply to this benefit performance

---

[1] *The Memoirs of Tate Wilkinson*, 1790, vol. iii, pp. 1–10.

story.[1] A common belief at the time was that Whitefield was merely an actor and therefore a hypocrite, and it was often suggested that he ran a kind of one-man theatre in opposition to the regular ones in London. In a twelve-page pamphlet in verse, entitled—

A Letter of Expostulation from the Manager of the Theatre in Tottenham Court Road to the Manager of the Theatre in the Hay Market,

the author, calling himself Squintum, the popular name for Whitefield, asks Foote, the actor-manager, to pool their resources. Both deal in Passions, says Squintum, and—

> The Passions alone, I find fit for my trade,
> The Passions are nat'ral, but morals were made.

Whitefield, however, preached dramatic sermons against the wickedness of the theatre. Once in 1753 he was preaching outside Glasgow and saw a kind of wooden booth being erected for a company of actors. He declaimed warmly against it and 'the consequence was, that before his departure workmen were being employed to take it down to prevent its being done by ruder hands'.[2] This contemporary account is of importance, because for the rest of the century the tale is so often repeated with wild exaggerations.[3] A few months after this removal of a booth at the fair, the story was retold in the *Newcastle Journal*. George Whitefield read it and wrote a reply, which was published on August 17, 1753:

NEWCASTLE.
August 17, 1753.

GENTLEMEN,—By your last Saturday's paper, I find that some Edinburgh correspondent has informed you, that when I was preaching at Glasgow on the 2nd inst. to a numerous audience, near the playhouse lately built, I inflamed the mob so much against it, that they ran directly from before me, and pulled it down to the ground; that several of the rioters, since then, have been taken up, and committed to jail. But I assure you this is mere slander and misinformation. It is true indeed, that I was preaching at Glasgow,

---

[1] See the account of *The Hypocrite* later in this chapter.
[2] *Scots Magazine*, vol. xv, p. 363.
[3] In *Some Account of the English Stage*, by J. Genest, 1832, vol. vii, p. 128, the general prejudice against theatres in Scotland is noted, but Methodists are not mentioned in particular.

to a numerous auditory at the beginning of this month; and that I thought it my duty to show the evil of having a playhouse erected in a trading city—almost, too, before the very door of the University. And this, by the help of God, if called to it, I should do again. But that I inflamed the mob, or that they ran directly from me, and pulled the playhouse down, or that the rioters were taken up and put into prison, is entirely false.

I suppose all this took its rise from the builder taking down the roof of the house himself. You must know that the walls of this playhouse were part of the old palace of the Bishop of Glasgow, and only had a board covering put upon them during the time of the players being there. They being gone, the owner (whether convinced of anything that was said, I cannot tell) began to take off the roof several days before I left that place; so that if there had been any riot doubtless I should have seen it. . . .

And therefore, if you please to inform the public and your Edinburgh correspondent of the mistake in to-morrow's paper, you will oblige, Gentlemen,

Your very humble servant,
GEORGE WHITEFIELD.

The story was not killed, however, and in *The History of the Scottish Stage*, by John Jackson, in 1793, an account of this incident is given, with Whitefield inspiring the weavers to attack and destroy a theatre in Glasgow.

In 1764 five gentlemen bought some ground to build another theatre there,[1] but so great was the Scottish dislike of the scheme that they could only secure it a mile outside the town and then by the enormous payment for those times of 5s. a square yard. 'If you erect a Temple of Belial', said the owner of the land, 'I shall expect an extraordinary sum for the purchase.'

Mrs. Bellamy, who was playing at Edinburgh, was to open the theatre and had sent her clothes and properties on ahead. The night before she arrived a mob went out to the new building, looted her goods, and burned the stage, all returning unrecognized. The fire was not discovered till the following day, when the managers and the magistrates offered a reward for any information. The *Scots Magazine* for April, 1764, has the following notice:

Some disorderly persons broke into the playhouse at Glasgow on April 24, and did considerable damage: 100 *l*. reward is offered by

[1] John Jackson, *op. cit.*

the magistrates and 50 *l.* by the managers of the theatre for discovering the rioters.[1]

Mrs. Bellamy, who was able to act on an improvised stage and with borrowed clothes, wrote an account to Tate Wilkinson at York,[2] and afterwards included it in her memoirs.[3] She asserted that a Methodist preacher incited his followers to do this. The story was afterwards repeated by other actors and foes of Methodism, but as Mrs. Bellamy was not present when the fire occurred and admits herself that no one saw the rioters or ever gave any information, it seems to rest on such flimsy foundations that little regard can be given to it. The Methodist Society in Glasgow at the time consisted of sixty-seven members.[4]

It is sometimes asserted that Whitefield's sermons against playhouses caused the actors to retaliate, but whether or not this claim is true, about 1760 plays satirizing Whitefield began to appear.[5] In that year, Samuel Foote at the Haymarket Theatre produced his play, *The Minor*.[6] In the three acts he played the parts of Shift, Smirke, and Mrs. Cole. The last is the only character of life or interest, but the criticism of the play centred upon her. She is a procuress who claims to have been converted by Dr. Squintum at the Tabernacle.

[1] *Scots Magazine*, vol. xxvi, p. 230.

[2] *Memoirs of Tate Wilkinson*, vol. iii, p. 130.

[3] *An Apology for the Life of George Anne Bellamy, late of Covent Garden Theatre*, six vols., 1785.

[4] Genest, *Some Account of the English Stage*, 1832, vol. vii, p. 128, says the stage only was injured: 'It was supposed to have been set on fire wilfully by some enthusiasts.' These detailed accounts of trivial incidents are included because the same stories have been repeated in recent years.

[5] Wesley, however, noted that at Newcastle in 1743, the Edinburgh Company of Comedians acted a farce, *Trick upon Trick; or Methodism Displayed*. See *Journal*, vol. iii, p. 110.

[6] Samuel Foote (1720–77) first tried his *Minor* at Crow Street Theatre, Dublin, on January 28, 1760. In this play of two acts, he played Shift, a character designed to satirize his associate, Tate Wilkinson. The play failed and he returned to the Haymarket and enlarged *The Minor* to three acts. A doubtful story repeated in *The Dictionary of National Biography* says Foote sent his play to the Archbishop of Canterbury with a request that he would alter anything that was objectionable, but nothing was changed. The reviews were not so kind, and suggested that much ought to have been omitted. The *Monthly Review*, for example, in July, 1760, said: 'Who can forbear smiling . . . with contempt for the author of such improbable scandal.' Many stories about *The Minor* appear in *Memoirs of Samuel Foote*, by William Cooke, three vols., 1805.

She justifies her villainy by quotations from his sermons, claiming that it is faith and not works that matters. Almost every sentence of her conversation contains his name. In the Introduction to the first scene, Foote himself appeared and talked with a character called Canker about the contents of the scenes about to be acted:

Foote: What think you of one of those itinerant field orators? . . .
Canker: Have a care. Dangerous ground. *Ludere cum sacris,* you know.
Foote: Now I look upon it in a different manner. I consider these gentlemen in the light of public performers, like myself: and whether we exhibit at Tottenham-Court, or the Haymarket, our purpose is the same, and the place is immaterial.

Later, Foote, as Mrs. Cole, explained her conversion:

Oh, it was a wonderful work! There had I been tossing in a sea of sin without rudder or compass; and had not the good gentleman piloted me into the harbour of grace, I must have struck against the rocks of reprobation and have been quite swallowed up in the whirlpool of despair. He was the precious instrument of my spiritual sprinkling. . . . If your mind be set upon a young country thing, to-morrow night, I believe I can furnish you.

Cole continues to praise Dr. Squintum:

Oh, he is a dear man! But for him I had been a lost sheep; never known the comforts of the new birth.

She is troubled, however, about the spiritual welfare of some of her charges:

The black-eyed girl is a merry little tit. A thousand pities she's such a reprobate!—But she'll mend; her time is not come: all shall have their call, as Mr. Squintum says, sooner or later; regeneration is not the work of a day. No, no, no.

After discoursing on her troubles, little worries of magistrates and prisons, she reflects;

However, it is a comfort, after all, to think one has passed through the world with credit and character. Ah! a good name, as Mr. Squintum says, is better than a gallipot of ointment.

She goes out to visit the preacher:

We are to have, at the tabernacle, an occasional hymn with a thanksgiving sermon for my recovery.

Though there is a certain amount of wit in this odious character, there is much truth in the review given the play by *Lloyd's Evening Post* for July 14, 1760:

How educated and respectable people could listen to such ribald and blasphemous outpourings, it is difficult to imagine. The whole thing is so steeped in lewdness, that it would be criminal even to reproduce the plot.

Fierce controversy was aroused by the play. Letters were sent to the reviews and many pamphlets published. Foote himself replied to one of these attacks,[1] admitting that it was hardly fair to satirize Whitefield for squinting which he could not help, but defending his choice of him as a subject for satire. It certainly can be argued that any words proceeding from the mouth of such an odious character as Mrs. Cole would do little harm to any honest man. There seems, however, to have been an epilogue in which Squintum himself appeared, and how libellous this was it is difficult to discover, because it is not included in Foote's works.

Another play, *The Register Office*,[2] by J. Reed, was produced the same year. This had much the same plot; the procuress, Mrs. Snarewell, talking about her friend, Dr. Watchlight, at the Tabernacle: 'Oh, he's a good creature, Mr. Gulwell—I must have been in a state of utter darkness but for him.' She also sings tunes used by Whitefield to a 'hymn' called 'Whenas a sinner groaneth sore'. An advertisement at the end of the 1761 edition of the play stated that this was not copied from *The Minor*, but had been in Foote's hands three years before.

In 1760 appeared another play, *The Methodist*, 'being a Continuation and Completion of the Plan of *The Minor*'. This was probably written by Israel Pottinger, though it is often ascribed to Foote.[3] As far as can be discovered, this was

[1] *A Letter from Mr. Foote to the Reverend Author of the 'Remarks Critical and Christian on "The Minor"'* , London, 1760. The unknown author replied.

[2] This play was produced at Drury Lane on April 23, 1761. Two characters, Lady Wrinkle and Mrs. Snarewell, were suppressed by the stage censor, but the unexpurgated piece was published. He introduced a new character, Mrs. Doggerel, and made other changes when the farce was revived in February, 1768. It was acted many other times during the century. (See Genest's *Account of the Stage* and 'Joseph Reed' in *D.N.B.*)

[3] Baker's *Biographia Dramatica* and the *D.N.B.* attribute this to Israel Pottinger.

not acted because it was too libellous. Dr. Squintum appears with Mrs. Cole and encourages her in her work, while she justifies her conduct with the words: 'The doctor knows that Works are of no consequence towards a future state, and that Faith is all.' In 1768 appeared *The Hypocrite;*[1] *a Comedy, taken from Molière and Cibber,* which has many Methodist references as well as allusions to public opinion at the time. In this Dr. Cantwell seems to represent a mixture of the Wesleys and George Whitefield, and old Lady Lambert to resemble Lady Huntingdon. In the fifth scene, she says to a servant:

Charles, step up into my study; bring down a dozen more of those manuals of devotion with the last hymns I composed; and, when he calls, give them to Mr. Mawworm; and, do you hear, if anyone inquires for me, say I am gone to Newgate and the Marshalsea, to distribute alms.

Scene vi is particularly interesting, because there seems to be a reference to the Shuter benefit performance. The old lady hotly denies that she has just been to a sinful play:

Dr. Cantwell: A playhouse is the devil's hot-bed.
Col. Lambert: And yet, Doctor, I have known some of the leaders of your tribe, as scrupulous as they are, who have been willing to gather fruit there for the use of the brethren—as in the case of a benefit.
Dr. Cantwell: The charity covereth the sin.

The audience of the time obviously was expected to understand the allusion.

There were a few other plays between 1760 and 1770 with slight attacks on Whitefield, and a large number of pamphlets on the subject soon appeared. One was written in reply to Whitefield's sermons on the stage by an anonymous author purporting to be a Methodist and defending plays and actors.

John Wesley was hardly mentioned in the controversy at all, though he made one allusion to it in a letter to *Lloyd's Evening Post* on November 17, 1760. He was answering an anonymous letter that had attacked various points of

[1] By Isaac Bickerstaffe, 1735–*c.*1812.

Methodism and had claimed that 'we had made them a theatrical scoff, and the common jest and scorn of every choirister in the streets'. The writer had expressed a wish for a court of judicature to give justice to such characters as Methodists. Wesley dealt with his theological arguments, expressed the view that the writer was an actor, and then referred to the desired court of justice:

Why do you wish for that you have already? The Court is erected; the holy, devout playhouse is become the House of Mercy, and does take cognizance hereof 'of all pretenders to sanctity, and happily furnishes us with a discerning spirit to distinguish betwixt right and wrong'. But I do not stand to their sentence; I appeal to Scripture and reason, and by these alone consent to be judged.[1]

Possibly the first writer was Foote himself, though there is little evidence for this view except that he was writing pamphlets against Whitefield at this time. At the time of the production of *The Minor*, Foote had had some fears about its production, because Mrs. Rich, the wife of the manager of Covent Garden Theatre, was a Methodist and a follower of Charles Wesley in particular.[2] As the years went on, she became increasingly friendly with Charles Wesley and did much to encourage his brilliant children and to secure the best training for them. Charlotte Rich, her daughter, married John Beard, a famous actor and singer, for whom Handel wrote the tenor parts of *The Messiah*, and he, too, was interested in the children, aiding them with advice and books. Beard was a friendly and popular man and became the manager of Covent Garden Theatre after the death of Rich.

After 1770 the anti-Methodist references on the stage seem to have become much fewer. This may have been due in part to the friendship of Charles Wesley with Mrs. Rich, Beard, and David Garrick, and of Whitefield with Shuter and some other actors, but it was also due to the growing prestige of John Wesley. As time went on, he was respected for his sincerity and was in favour with Government circles on account of his attitude towards the American War.

[1] *Letters*, vol. iv, p. 111.
[2] See *Memoirs of Tate Wilkinson*, vol. iii.

Possibly Methodism had also lost its novelty for satire and was becoming an accepted part of English life. Actors and actresses like Tate Wilkinson and Mrs. Bellamy published memoirs towards the end of the century in which they ridiculed Methodists with the old stories of hypocrisy, and attacks on actors that have been described already. In connexion with Mrs. Bellamy, it is interesting to note that Wesley a year before he died read her *Life*. He says:

> I retired to Peckham, and at leisure hours read part of a very pretty trifle—the Life of Mrs. Bellamy.[1] Surely never did any since Dryden, study more—
> 'To make vice pleasing, and damnation shine'—than this lively and elegant writer. . . . Abundance of anecdotes she inserts, which may be true or false. One of them, concerning Mr. Garrick, is curious. She says: 'When he was taking ship for England, a lady presented him with a parcel, which she desired him not to open till he was at sea. When he did, he found Wesley's *Hymns*, which he immediately threw overboard.' I cannot believe it. I think Mr. Garrick had more sense. He knew my brother well; and he knew him to be not only far superior in learning, but in poetry, to Mr. Thomson and all his theatrical writers put together.[2]

After examining the attitude of the Wesleys and Whitefield towards plays, it is interesting to look through the *Lives of Early Methodist Preachers*, where there are a number of accounts of play readings and attendance at playhouses. Several writers describe how wicked they felt, when as young men and long before they met any Methodists, they went to a theatre. To take only one example: Thomas Tennant, a Norfolk man, came to London and heard Wesley preach at the Foundry. He writes:

> Before this I had been exceedingly fond of going to plays, yet never went without a dread upon my spirits. When I was there, I always seemed as one treading on forbidden ground; and particularly one night, when two persons were trampled to death, in crowding up the same passage which I had but just before got up. I also took great delight in reading plays; for which purpose I collected a number of the best I could meet with, and often pleased myself and my companions with the repetition of some of the most striking passages in

---

[1] *An Apology for the Life of George Anne Bellamy*, six vols., 1785. She died in 1788.

[2] *Journal*, vol. viii, p. 34.

them. . . . At last, from a full conviction of this, I committed all my plays to the flames and determined to spend my leisure hours in reading more profitable books.[1]

In the nineteenth century appeared an interesting little book entitled *Memoir of Mr. John Dungett of Newcastle-on-Tyne*, by J. Heaton. John Dungett was born at Gateshead in 1780, and died in 1833. His father was an innkeeper and fairly well-off, but his mother was interested in Methodism and frequently took her son to the Orphan House at Newcastle. He was apprenticed to a surgeon for four years, but, finding he had a fine voice and was fond of singing, he abandoned this and joined a company of actors who toured about the country. The author then says:

How long he continued with this 'corps dramatique' I am not aware, as he was by no means forward to refer, even to his most intimate friends, to this part of his history, so painful was the remembrance of it to his renewed mind. . . .

And here I cannot forbear mentioning his opinion of the immorality of theatrical amusements; although he thought highly as a man of letters and refined taste of the literary beauties of Shakespeare, and some other dramatic writers, yet he had the utmost horror of the evil tendencies of dramatic representation, and particularly the vile and blasphemous trash found in the productions of our modern stage writers. . . .

He had been behind the scenes, and knew well the abominations of the theatre, and especially its utter inadequacy as a medium of moral instruction. He had seen the monster without its mask, and he was not backward to declare its features to be awful and hideous.[2]

Thus John Dungett left the wicked life of the stage and chose the most virtuous of vocations, that of a schoolmaster.

This account of John Dungett is particularly interesting, not only as illustrating the loss in the nineteenth century of much of the earlier spontaneity and vigour of Methodist biography and its replacement too often by heavy moralizations, but also for the increasing dislike of theatrical entertainments. This is shown again in an article in the *Methodist Magazine* for 1799, which is extracted chiefly 'from an ancient

[1] *Lives of Early Methodist Preachers*, vol. iii, pp. 428–9.
[2] I am indebted to the Rev. F. F. Bretherton, B.A., for lending me this book.

writer on stage exhibitions'. At the end of the extracts fiercely attacking the morality of the stage, the compiler writes a final paragraph and says:

It may be presumed, that no Methodist frequents the theatre, but as numbers of those who read the *Methodist Magazine* are not of our Society . . . this discourse may not be improper.

He ends by admitting that the theatre of the day was much better than previously, but asks three questions:

> Is the playhouse a proper school of virtue?
> Is it a way of glorifying God?
> Is money spent there well laid out?[1]

Thus, while the earlier Methodists probably seldom went to a theatre after their conversion, they may occasionally have done so, but the Methodists at the end of the century and at the beginning of the nineteenth century would not have permitted it for a moment. It was assumed naturally that 'no Methodist attends a theatre', and that their centres of social life were in their own societies and homes. In doing this they moved into the position of the Nonconformists, who had always disliked the stage. It might be suggested that the numbers of Dissenters who joined the Methodists in the second half of the century increased Methodist antagonism towards theatres, but the explanation is more likely to be that as many became more serious they withdrew from the pomps and vanity of the wicked world. In their minds the stage was closely connected with this and with the sinful lusts of the flesh.

The earlier Methodist was satirized on the stage and often met with actors and players at booths in fairs. When he turned for guidance in his attitude towards pleasures, he received advice like the following from Wesley:

I am convinced as true religion or holiness cannot be without cheerfulness . . . and that true religion has nothing sour, austere, unsociable in it. . . . Are you for having as much cheerfulness as you can? So am I. Do you endeavour to keep alive your taste for all the truly innocent pleasures of life? So do I likewise. Do you refuse no

[1] *Methodist Magazine*, 1799, p. 596.

pleasure but what is a hindrance to some greater good or has a tendency to some evil? It is my very rule.[1]

In the nineteenth century Methodism tended to be more self-contained and too often to expend its energies within its own fold, so that for a hundred years there would be little to say at all about Methodists and theatres. It was a pity; for it was probably a more healthy sign for both when they were more intermingled, even if hostile, in the previous century.

---

[1] *Letters*, vol. i, pp. 218–19. See also Luke Tyerman: *The Oxford Methodists*, pp. 173–5.

METHODISM AS SEEN IN THE LITERATURE OF
THE AGE

ANTI-METHODIST WRITERS: Bishop Lavington, Lord Bolingbroke, Bishop Warburton, A. M. Toplady, the *Gospel Magazine*, the *Weekly Miscellany*, the *Gentleman's Magazine*, the *Monthly Review*, the *London Magazine*. PROSE REFERENCES: Richard Graves: *The Spiritual Quixote*. James Lackington: *Memoirs, Confessions*. Smollett: *Humphry Clinker*. Fielding, Goldsmith, Sterne, Walpole, Dr. Johnson. VERSE REFERENCES: Pope, Churchill, Robert Lloyd, Chatterton. Anstey: *New Bath Guide*. Smart, Cowper, Blake.